"I am often asked to endorse a book or movie on near-death experiences. Out of courtesy I read them all, but only rarely do I give my personal endorsement and preference. I am pleased to tell you this is one of those rare occasions.

"Dr. Kathy Boyls and her husband, Steve, have given life to the story of Steve's death in this beautiful book of love, perseverance, faith, and proof of a miracle! His description and details brought back to me so many memories of my journey through death and subsequent return. I think that God tailors each heavenly experience to the relevance of the life we lived on Earth. The description of the flowers and beauty of Heaven and Steve's visit with the horses in Paradise delighted me, and I felt the joy once again of my experience.

"The most delightful surprise of this book was the similarity of Kathy's devoted advocating and prayer for Steve to my wife Lorraine's prayers for me beseeching Jesus that 'if it be your will, please send Jim back.'

"In these dark days that surround us, this book will inspire your faith in God and in the unrelenting love of a wife for the love of her life."

James D. Woodford, author, *Heaven: An Unexpected Journey*

"If you have ever wondered, *God, where are you?* then this book is for you. *I've Been to Heaven* will convince you that we serve a God who is living and active and involved in the affairs of our lives. This book captured my attention from the very first page through the final words. Steve and Kathy Boyls's story must seem hard to believe, but I can assure you that every word of it is true. *I've Been to Heaven* will encourage you to believe that miracles still happen today."

Carol McLeod, author, Bible teacher, podcaster, blogger

"The vivid account of Steve Boyls's trip to Heaven and Kathy Boyls's work on Earth as a team is awe inspiring. *I've Been to Heaven* captures the heart of God as seen through Steve's heavenly encounters, balanced delicately by Kathy's spiritual and natural efforts in battling for her husbands' life on Earth. The reader is confronted with answers of Heaven's inner workings in very practical ways.

"This work also illustrates the power of love between husband and wife in life's battles and challenges that we all face. As a neurosurgeon who has encountered many life-and-death situations, I really appreciate the gravity of the real-life events that took place as described in this work. This book is a must-read for those who want to know more about Heaven's inner workings as well as how partnership and perseverance can positively impact the most dismal of situations. Congratulations on this inspirational piece!"

Avery M. Jackson III, MD, neurosurgeon trustee and founder, The Body Healthcare; author, *The God Prescription*

"*I've Been to Heaven* is a powerful, Spirit-filled testimony that transcends the veil between Earth and eternity. Steve and Kathy Boyls, together with award-winning journalist Troy Anderson, deliver a captivating and deeply personal account of divine encounters, miraculous moments, and the undeniable reality of Heaven. This book will stir your faith, ignite your hope, and challenge you to see life—and the afterlife—through a heavenly lens. A must-read for anyone seeking a deeper understanding of God's eternal promises and the supernatural realm that awaits us. This book will change your life!"

Pastor Paul Begley

"I come from a family that is passionate about evangelizing and sharing the gospel of Jesus Christ. One man told my father about Jesus, and it changed the history of my family forever. My dad has spent the last sixty-four years sharing the life-changing miracle of Jesus Christ. We believe in miracles. This book shows a similar passion that drives Kathy and Steve as they write their story of healing, power, and hope.

"For followers of Jesus, Heaven is the ultimate eternal goal, but while we are on this Earth, we have to share our stories and bring Jesus to those who have given up and have no hope for their future. Jesus' healing power is real, prayers of the saints are necessary, and we must be generous with our love and the words of our testimonies that will encourage and help others to not shrink from death."

Alicia Cruz Dow, Nicky Cruz Outreach

I'VE BEEN
TO
HEAVEN

Other Books by Troy Anderson

with Col. David J. Giammona

The Military Guide to Armageddon
The Military Guide to Disarming Deception
Your Mission in God's Army

I'VE BEEN
═══ TO ═══
HEAVEN

The True Story of a Husband's Supernatural
Near-Death Experience of the Afterlife,
His Wife's Prayer That Brought Him Back, and
God's Message of Hope for the World

Steve and Kathy Boyls, MD
and Troy Anderson

Chosen
a division of Baker Publishing Group
Minneapolis, Minnesota

Published by Chosen Books
Minneapolis, Minnesota
ChosenBooks.com

Chosen Books is a division of
Baker Publishing Group, Grand Rapids, Michigan

Printed in the United States of America

Library of Congress Cataloging-in-Publication Data

Names: Boyls, Steve, author. | Boyls, Kathy, author. | Anderson, Troy (Journalist), author.
Title: I've been to heaven : the true story of a husband's supernatural near-death experience of the afterlife, his wife's prayer that brought him back, and God's message of hope for the world / Steve and Kathy Boyls and Troy Anderson.
Description: Minneapolis, Minnesota : Chosen, a division of Baker Publishing Group, [2025] | Includes bibliographical references.
Identifiers: LCCN 2025002736 | ISBN 9780800773328 (paperback) | ISBN 9780800773359 | ISBN 9781493452279 (ebook)
Subjects: LCSH: Boyls, Steve. | Christian biography—United States. | Near-death experiences—Religious aspects—Christianity. | Death—Religious aspects—Christianity. | Future life—Christianity. | LCGFT: Autobiographies.
Classification: LCC BR1725.B674 A3 2025 | DDC 270.092 [B]—dc23/eng/20250314
LC record available at https://lccn.loc.gov/2025002736

Cover design by Dan Pitts

The Author is represented by the literary agency of BurnsLaw PC.

Baker Publishing Group publications use paper produced from sustainable forestry practices and postconsumer waste whenever possible.

25 26 27 28 29 30 31   7 6 5 4 3

Steve and Kathy

We dedicate this book to those mighty prayer warriors who made an Ephesians 6:11 stand with us while Steve was in the hospital. Our hearts are overwhelmed with gratitude for your incredible kindness and unyielding faith in the power of our Almighty God. You demonstrated how the body of Christ is designed to function.

Troy

I dedicate this book first and foremost to my Lord and Savior Jesus Christ, whose grace, power, and faithfulness have been evident throughout this journey. I also dedicate it to Steve and Kathy Boyls, whose inspirational stories and steadfast faith and wisdom have been a true blessing in our lives, and to my amazing wife, Irene.

Contents

Foreword

SHARON DAUGHERTY

Two highly educated people found themselves in an incredible experience: Steve battled COVID and went to Heaven as Kathy prayed to keep him here on Earth.

Steve gives an amazing description of Heaven to encourage believers with what they can look forward to and expect to see. He explains there are many similarities between Earth and Heaven. We will "not be fat babies floating on clouds." We will be in the prime of life. We will encounter those who passed on before us, even babies who died at birth. We will recognize our loved ones when we see them.

Heaven will be beautiful, and we will be happy to be there. There will be flowers and trees, birds and animals, rivers, lakes, mountains, and fields. Steve likes baseball, and there was a baseball game when he was there. There will be no time and no stress, but peace, joy, and love will dominate the atmosphere. There will be no sickness, no one lacking anything physically. We will experience life without the curse that is on the Earth.

Jesus will be the one we desire to see more than anything or anyone.

Steve and Kathy address many challenges faced by people who are in need of healing and God's resurrection power. Their covenant relationship with God was something they drew upon for Steve's healing. Each had to choose not to allow their education to rob their faith in believing God for Steve's miracle.

Steve and Kathy want people to know that Heaven is very real. Those who have accepted Jesus Christ as Lord and Savior spend eternity in Heaven with Him. Jesus gave His life for us to be connected to God, who created us to choose to know Him personally.

You'll discover how to believe God and His Word and to continue standing in faith for His promises. Steve and Kathy's resilient faith in the Lord is inspiring. As you read you'll be pointed back to Jesus and encouraged to believe God in all circumstances.

I highly recommend *I've Been to Heaven*.

Sharon Daugherty, founding pastor,
Victory Church

Foreword

JANIE DAIGLE

My brother Steve went to Heaven. When he revealed this to me, he said he wanted me to hear about it from him, not from another person. He didn't want me to think he was crazy.

With a story like his, many will say we don't have evidence that it happened—not the kind of evidence we can examine. As a retired attorney, I'm all about that kind of evidence. But my life experiences have taught me that the things of God can't be viewed through the lens of the world or even what we know as facts or any evidence we do have. Faith is required.

So when Steve came to my house and told me that at some point while he was hospitalized with COVID-19 he went to Heaven, I knew faith would be what helped me understand what he went through. You can't inspect this story in the way you would a court case. To understand, acknowledge, and believe Steve requires faith in something you can't see.

I learned a lot about the faith walk during my brother's fight to stay alive. When he was in the hospital, I had a team of friends and pastors from California praying for us, and I can honestly attest that I had never prayed that much in my whole life. It was a constant battle, praying daily for Steve's physical condition to improve, for his life to be spared while he was on the ventilator.

And praying and learning didn't stop after the ventilator.

He still had a long way to go.

It was a roller coaster.

Steve would be doing really well, and then something would happen and he'd go downhill. The doctors and nurses told us that, for a lot of people, the progression of this disease is that they improve, you think they're doing fine, and then they're suddenly down again.

But Steve just kept coming back. From the ventilator, from three bouts of pneumonia, from being unable to walk, he kept fighting—and God kept working. The hand of God was on my brother. Steve's survival of COVID and many setbacks all while being spiritually attacked day after day is a miracle. We have doctors and nurses and medicines and machines to help us, but God is the ultimate Healer.

"People may think I'm nuts for saying this, or they may think it was just the drugs I was on," my brother explained, "but it wasn't. It was a totally different experience."

Steve told me about the angel Marzuka and the scenery and the Welcome Center in Heaven. He told me about seeing our brother, Ted, who was killed in 1991. Ted was such a wonderful person, always laughing and telling corny jokes, and he was taken so suddenly at the age of forty-one. But there he was in Heaven, and they went to a baseball game together—both are big baseball fans.

Steve recognized our parents and said they looked young and healthy. He saw our grandmother and our niece. He even saw his unborn son, Daniel.

All of it was uplifting and hope-filled.

As you think about this story, know that the God who created everything created Heaven. It's real. And know that He is in control. Humanity thinks we're in control of everything, like the climate and even the future. But COVID showed us we're not. We impact things, but we don't control them. Only God, who is outside of time and space, can truly help us. There's great comfort in that fact.

When I read a few books about other people going to and returning from Heaven, I thought, God created the universe, it's His domain, and there's nothing He can't do. So if He wants to bring somebody to Heaven and then send them back to tell their story to glorify Him, He can certainly do that.

I believe my brother was sent back to tell us this story. As Jesus told him—after he came home from his hospitalizations—Steve is a "messenger of hope." So if you're really seeking, let his story touch your soul, get into your heart, and fill you with hope. Let the Holy Spirit move in your life, because this life is not the end. There is eternal peace and happiness in Heaven with God.

You hold in your hands a firsthand account from someone I've known my entire life. Steve is a devout believer and has no reason to fabricate a story like this. After hearing him out, questioning him, and looking at the detail he presented, I believe him.

Steve Boyls went to Heaven and came back.

Janie Daigle

Introduction

A Regular Guy's Amazing Journey

STEVE BOYLS

I didn't ask to go to Heaven. In fact, I'd never thought about going there until after I die. And although some of my family and friends have passed on to this wonderful place, I'd never really thought about what Heaven is like. In addition, I was never really interested in hearing or reading about the experiences of others who had gone to Heaven and come back to talk about it.

But now I've been to Heaven myself. And it's real and tangible, filled with life, light, and beauty so incredible that our most celebrated places on this planet pale in comparison. The breathtaking scenes I experienced there are well described in Scripture, like the Throne Room (Revelation 4), the streets of gold (Revelation 21:21), and the "river of water of life" (Revelation 22:1), which we often simply call the River of Life. And 1 Corinthians 2:9–10 tells us, "Eye has not seen, nor ear heard, nor have entered into the heart of man the things which God has prepared for those who love Him. But God has revealed them to us through His Spirit. For the Spirit searches all things, yes, the deep things of God." I can truly say that the places I visited in Heaven, the eternal home God has prepared for us, were beyond what my natural mind could even imagine. And by His grace, He revealed them to me.

My journey began during my stay in the ICU (Intensive Care Unit) at a hospital near our home in Tulsa, Oklahoma, after contracting COVID. While my wife, Kathy, and many others prayed fervently for me every day of my three-month hospitalization, they were completely unaware of the spiritual journey I took and the fascinating revelation granted me. I describe my journey there as my spirit separated from my physical body and traveled through Earth's atmosphere and the cosmos to this wondrous place called Heaven.

And then I came back.

I've always considered myself "just a regular guy," no one special or particularly gifted. I've worked as a software engineer most of my life, enjoyed spending time with my family and friends, and attended church regularly. And although I'd given my life to Christ many years ago, I'd never felt a calling to any type of ministry. So it's amazing to me that God would choose this vessel to reveal His glory and recount in detail the following scenes of Heaven.

1

Unexpected Crisis

KATHY

Heal me, Lord, and I will be healed; save me and I will be saved, for you are the one I praise.

Jeremiah 17:14 NIV

It was late November 2021, and our Oklahoma weather was starting to cool off as fall was in the air. Steve hadn't been sick with anything in almost two years, and we'd just visited a few potential colleges with our younger daughter, Stacie. But now he wasn't feeling well.

We didn't know he had COVID-19.

As a medical doctor, I was ever vigilant in washing my hands before and after seeing every patient in the office. And I'd always safeguarded our family by washing up and changing clothes when I came home before embracing them, cooking for them, or doing anything around the house. This routine drastically reduced the germs between my patients, me, and my family. And none of us had ever had COVID.

We think Steve might have been exposed to COVID during one of his weekly physical therapy sessions following carpal tunnel surgery for his right hand earlier in the month. First he was unable to shake a cough, congestion, and fatigue. Then after a few days, what he thought was just a nasty cold started affecting his chest. With a history of asthma, Steve was familiar with using his inhaler when a cold could jeopardize his breathing. A seasoned software engineer, he treated the symptoms and continued working diligently despite how he felt.

His birthday was approaching, and his determination to shake the illness and enjoy some time with family drove him to finish a software project for Pastor Paul Begley's app, Apocalypse Watch. He was writing an update and wanted to release a new version as soon as possible. In truth, he thought he'd rounded a corner. But I needed more convincing, so I watched him closely.

When we went out for Steve's birthday and dined at one of his favorite restaurants, P. F. Chang's, I noticed he wasn't himself. He was trying to enjoy the dinner, but I could tell he was tired. He was also coughing and still stuffed up. Stacie and Steve's sister, Janie, had come with us. It was fun, but Steve's appetite could have been better.

Janie noticed he was struggling as well. When she asked him about it, he played it down (like a lot of men would).

"Oh, I'm okay," he told her. "It's just a cold. It's just a cold."

When they brought a sparkler and dessert for Steve to celebrate, he enjoyed it but said he wished he felt better. This was concerning. Steve is normally quite a character! He's always upbeat and has acquired the label of "eternal optimist." He sees the glass as half full while I tend to see it as half empty. When we were first married, Steve always woke up in a good mood and whistled in the mornings. I, on the other hand, moaned and asked for coffee. In my defense, at the time I was a resident in Pediatrics with one-hundred-hour workweeks and little sleep.

God knew we needed each other. Steve is always encouraging me when things go wrong. He has quite a sense of humor and makes me laugh a lot. When I was younger, my mother knew I was too serious and needed to laugh more. So I joked with her that I would marry a clown who would keep me laughing the rest of my life.

Sometimes I don't realize Steve's joking with me and I take what he says too seriously, but he definitely keeps me laughing. We've been told we complete each other, fitting together like two pieces in a puzzle. Steve is also the classic dad joke teller. He's never at a loss for a joke and always loved trying to embarrass our girls in front of their friends.

For Steve, the days following that birthday dinner were a blur. Janie checked in with him a few times, but he told her he was doing fine.

"Well, maybe you should get tested," she said. "Maybe you've got COVID."

Steve responded, "Nah, I don't have COVID."

On December 3, just after the stitches from his surgery had been removed that day, he left me a voicemail saying he was starting to feel better despite the lingering cough and fatigue. I had just started to feel sick that day myself, and he also prayed for me to feel well. But as he ended the call, the illness he'd considered waning was about to rise with a vengeance.

Decision Time

The next day Stacie and I were both tired and suffering from headaches. I grew concerned, thinking we needed to test for COVID. So we all three took a home test the following day, December 5.

We all had it.

I let Janie know we'd tested positive and advised her to take the test when she said she wasn't feeling well either. She said she would. Then I consulted a physician friend of mine who had successfully treated many outpatient COVID patients. I started us on a daily regimen of vitamins C and D, zinc, and other immune-supporting supplements and medicines. Working from home, Steve kept on programming. I took off from my practice for a week that extended into two.

Thankfully, I had no respiratory symptoms while I was sick. Unlike Stacie and Steve, my symptoms were confined to my head. It was the worst headache of my life, and I thought my head might explode. I hardly ever get headaches, so this was unusual for me. But it was the beginning of my "COVID vacation." Bummer!

Stacie, with reasonably mild respiratory symptoms, stayed home from school. She was eighteen at the time, a senior in high school focusing on studying violin for college the following year. A beautiful girl with dark hair and hazel eyes, she accepted Jesus at a very young age—three or four—and was filled with the Holy Spirit at age four. She had numerous angelic visitations and saw her "music angel" when she was young.

Stacie and I slowly improved that first week of our illness (and our bodies grew stronger over the second week), but Steve got worse over those four days after we all tested positive. Much later I learned he'd stopped taking the supplements and medicines because he not only believed some of the medications gave him diarrhea but thought he was feeling better.

Steve developed lower respiratory symptoms, so we bought a pulse oximeter at Walgreens to test his oxygen levels. I was proactive and doing all the right things, but Steve's stubbornness made his condition worse. I gave him nebulized budesonide and nebulized albuterol as this infection triggered his asthma. But his oxygen saturation continued to drop, and he needed supplemental oxygen. We called his primary care physician, Dr. Jeff, and requested that an oxygen concentrator be delivered to our home. Dr. Jeff was on top of it and got it there quickly.

Stacie really wanted Steve to go to the hospital, even while I was still feeling awful and wondered if I might have a stroke. I also had a tough time thinking straight and was unsure if my judgment was the best. And I didn't sleep much as I was giving Steve breathing treatments and constantly watching his oxygen level. But his breathing grew more difficult, and it was increasingly challenging to keep his oxygen saturation up even with the oxygen concentrator. We were concerned. The saturation would improve at home if he would lie on his stomach, but he didn't want to; he couldn't get comfortable in that position.

Finally, four days after we all tested positive, Stacie came into our bedroom and said she'd prayed and felt we needed to take her dad to the hospital.

I was concerned too. Steve's oxygen saturation was down to 85 percent, much less than the normal 95 percent or higher, and I wanted to do the best thing for him. I thought he might need a few days of CPAP or BiPAP (a mask that provides continuous or intermittent pressure to keep one's airways open). We took Steve to the hospital on December 9, nine days after he started getting sick. I texted our dear friends of more than thirty years, Steve and Marilyn, who live overseas, and let them know I was taking my Steve to the hospital. Stacie messaged her sister to tell her we were taking him in as well.

We had no idea what was going to happen when we got there.

Losing Control

The weather was dreary and getting colder, the afternoon sky gray and overcast. As we drove, Steve said he felt horrible, but he was his usual calm self. He thought the doctors and nurses would help him get well. He texted Pastor Begley and told him he was going to the hospital, saying he expected to be there a few days, not more than a week.

The hospital is only about ten to twelve minutes from our home, so I knew the small portable oxygen tank we took with us would last for the trip. But I called ahead and asked an ER nurse to have them hook Steve up to wall oxygen as soon as possible because what was in the portable tank wouldn't last much longer.

Pulling up to the ER entrance, I got as close as I could to the door since Steve couldn't walk very far due to his difficulty breathing. Steve and Stacie went right in, and I left to park the car. Steve and I didn't even say goodbye. I thought I would be with them momentarily, and I thought we could stay together, at least in the ER.

Later, Stacie said everything happened quickly and she felt a little numb the whole time.

When she and Steve entered the ER, the nurses told her neither of us could stay with her dad. Not only did we both have COVID as well, but no COVID patients were allowed visitors.

As Steve was taken away, for a moment there Stacie thought, *Wow, I hope that's not the last time I ever see my dad alive.*

Stacie called my cell phone and told me what happened, so I drove back to the ER entrance and picked her up. Later Steve told me he was put into a little room with four other people with COVID and was in there for ten minutes before they hooked him up to oxygen. After twenty minutes, Steve was taken to the ICU in a wheelchair.

As we headed home, some doubt crept in over whether it had been right to take Steve to the ER—none of us had any idea this separation would happen. And a little fear crept in as well. I was concerned that I couldn't be in the hospital to watch over his treatment. I'd never admitted a pediatric patient to the hospital for COVID, so I had no experience with inpatient COVID protocols—certainly not the ones they used in the ICU.

As Steve and I texted—one of us in the ICU and the other at home with a pounding headache—little did we know that, because of a hospital rule, we wouldn't see each other for the next twenty days and that our lives would be dramatically changed by all that was to follow.

2

The Earthly Journey Begins

KATHY

Praise the Lord, my soul, and forget not all his benefits—who forgives all your sins and heals all your diseases, who redeems your life from the pit and crowns you with love and compassion, who satisfies your desires with good things so that your youth is renewed like the eagle's.

Psalm 103:2–5

As a wife and physician, I've always tried to take good care of Steve without being overbearing.

For instance, Steve has had type 1 diabetes since he was twelve years old. When we started dating, he grew serious about his blood sugar control. He really impressed his endocrinologist, who had attempted to get Steve to take better care of himself for years. After we married, Steve took pride in how well he controlled his blood sugar, keeping his hemoglobin A1C (a measure of the hemoglobin that has sugar attached to it) around six units. That's excellent control for a diabetic.

In the first year of marriage, however, I had to learn how to help take care of Steve without being intrusive. One morning he started vomiting after taking his insulin. I was concerned his blood sugar would drop and he wouldn't be able to keep anything in his stomach, resulting in a very low blood sugar. I had to give him a shot of glucagon to bring it up. Instinctively, I tried to check his pulse—and discovered this wasn't the route I could take. He pulled back harshly, saying he'd taken care of himself for a long time and was not my patient. The need to tread lightly to gain his cooperation was evident. Steve did not want a doctor; he wanted a wife, first and foremost.

But he learned to take my medical suggestions when approached with patience, the emphasis on his having autonomy in his medical decisions while still allowing me to express my opinion diplomatically. We have an amazing understanding now, and the level of trust because of my medical judgment has only deepened and strengthened our love.

So for both of us, the hospital's rule allowing no visitors because of COVID was devastating. After thirty years of marriage and rarely being apart, twenty days cut off from Steve seemed like an eternity. Outside of a mission trip to Malaysia and a few business trips over the years, nothing had separated us for more than two weeks. We are true soulmates. And I had gone to many doctor appointments with him in the past. In fact, he asked me to go one time when he visited an endocrinologist who barely let Steve speak and talked a million miles an hour. I had to work at slowing the guy down and forcing him to explain things in a way Steve could understand.

What follows is what was going on in our earthly world, but in the next chapter, Steve will let you in on what was going on in the heavenly world he was entering.

Facing the Cons

Before taking Steve to the hospital, I had weighed the pros and cons—and the pros won. As I said in the last chapter, I thought a higher level of care than I could provide at home was probably necessary. But there were cons I didn't anticipate: being unable to visit Steve and watch over his care in the ICU, communication with the hospital staff based on their availability, and hospital protocols dictating certain medical care. As a pediatrician, I was also unfamiliar with the environment of the adult ICU. It was a formidable place where, we have now discovered, many dear souls spent their last moments on earth.

As a critical thinker, I don't just accept medical opinions; my education and experience allow me to critically evaluate medical decision-making and protocols. I like to see the evidence for myself. And with the COVID pandemic, I learned there were unusual and suspicious practices. I also knew the side effects of Remdesivir, and I'd told Steve, "Absolutely no Remdesivir!" I didn't think they could talk him into taking it, but in the state he was in—barely able to breathe, focused on living and nothing else—after about two days in the hospital, a pulmonologist had talked Steve into getting it.

It's one thing to be separated from the ones we love; it's another when that separation is forced for an arbitrary number of days with no scientific basis for the time frame. Not one to stay inactive, in the days following Steve's admission to the ICU I developed a new routine. I'd be up at 5:30 a.m. to call his nurse to learn what his morning labs were and how he did overnight.

At first Steve and I were able to talk by phone so he could convey how he was doing. Via text messages, he was even able to convey a sense of optimism, which most of us were fighting to maintain. But it became more difficult for him to talk once he was placed on the BiPAP mask.

My dear husband was in isolation in the ICU, and though this is where his supernatural story began, it was a time of stress for me. So many of my friends and family were a support, though, especially my friend Marilyn. Our constant text messaging got me through. I knew what prayer warriors she and her husband were and that they were praying Psalm 91 over all my family because Stacie and I needed to be completely healed. Marilyn encouraged me to *get the word of God going into his room all day. . . . The Word is powerful, and it will heal him. Even if he's not conscious, if he's sleeping, just keep it going. Try to get them to go with that.*

The Ventilator

After Steve was in the ICU for five days, Stacie and I were in the car together when the pulmonary physician called to tell me Steve was intubated urgently. Actually, he'd convinced Steve intubation and a ventilator would help his lungs heal, and Steve had consented.

I called Marilyn and Steve, and they prayed with me and encouraged me. So on December 14 Steve was intubated and placed on a ventilator.

"It was a leap of faith to trust the doctors," says Stacie, "that they would be able to wean him off of it eventually, because you hear ventilator, you think 'end of life support.'"

Certainly, Steve didn't fully understand what this meant for his bodily functions when he consented, and it was so hard not to be able to explain the whole picture to him.

After Steve was intubated, his isolation was not only physical but mental and emotional. To be separated from those you love in every aspect of life is both painful and heart-wrenching. This is why in Romans 8 the apostle Paul emphasizes that nothing can ever separate us from the love of God. Although the love of my life was alone in that room, he was never alone.

Intubation is the placement of an endotracheal tube into the mouth, down the throat, and through the vocal cords. There it sits, in the trachea, delivering breaths from the machine we call a ventilator, directly to the lungs. Over time, this forced air and the friction of the tube against the vocal cords can have unwanted consequences. However, sometimes a patient does need this system to maintain oxygenation through the lungs.

As a pediatrician, I've intubated many a newborn and am quite familiar with the process. Because the intubated patient must remain perfectly still both during the intubation and while on the ventilator, an intravenous drip containing a paralytic is started and continued until the patient is ready to be extubated (the endotracheal tube removed). Also, since the patient must be sedated to avoid "fighting" the ventilator, intravenous drips of sedatives are given. These are narcotics and other drugs that keep one in a medically induced coma. The ventilator is a machine that delivers volume or pressure to the lungs to maintain oxygenation and facilitate removal of carbon dioxide.

Other necessary medical procedures accompany intubation and ventilation. Since the patient can no longer receive nutrition by mouth, an orogastric tube is placed through the mouth, down the esophagus, and into the stomach to deliver liquid nutrition, hanging from a bag controlled by a pump, directly into the stomach. In addition, since the intubated patient doesn't have bladder control, a foley catheter must be placed and urine output must be accurately tracked. You can see that fluid balance and electrolytes become very important in this situation. There is also continuous monitoring of oxygen saturation, blood pressure, heart rate, and EKG rhythm. The patient's respiratory rate is controlled by the ventilator settings as they are no longer breathing on their own in this medically induced coma.

Since Steve has type 1 diabetes and wore an insulin pump as well as a continuous glucose monitor when he was intubated, he could no longer control his blood sugar with the pump and monitor. So the staff also had to monitor his blood sugar and give him insulin. For a few weeks, he was on a continuous insulin drip that had to be monitored carefully.

I've always taken care of my family's medical needs, and never have I felt so "out of the loop" in a family medical situation as when Steve was in the ICU. Communication with him was impossible at this point because he was sedated and paralyzed. It was as if he were totally gone from my life—from all our lives. Before he was intubated, we could at least text and occasionally speak. Once he was on the ventilator, he was unreachable. A certain aspect of grief occurs when all communication is cut off. It was devastating.

Even now, our hearts go out to family members who have loved ones in the hospital and can't understand the meaning of the medical jargon and what all the monitors, machines, and IV drips are telling them. Our experience gave me new insights into the plight of family members when their adult loved ones are in the ICU.

Again, our friends Marilyn and Steve were an invaluable support to me. Although they live overseas, they stayed in close contact and spent many sleepless nights praying for Steve. They often texted me things like *We're fighting with you. Steve has a covenant right to breathe freely. Lungs, be healed in Jesus' name.*

Julie and David Yoder, our friends from Sunday school, arranged many meals for Stacie and me and let me visit late at night to pray with them. Just being there to listen and encourage me as I cried helped me stay strong.

Then I reached a low point—my lowest point—on Friday, December 17.

An Embassy of Heaven

Two days earlier, during a time of prayer on the phone with Marilyn, she had a spiritual encounter with the Holy Spirit. She describes it this way:

> All of a sudden I was in our bedroom, but I was really in Tulsa. It's like the Lord opened my spiritual eyes and I saw Steve's hospital room. And God led me very strongly, "You decree that Steve's room is now called an embassy of Heaven."

So as we were praying, Marilyn decreed, "In Jesus' name, Steve's hospital room is now an embassy of Heaven." She later explained:

> As I was decreeing that, I saw a few huge angels posted at the door as well as one coming into his room, and that the enemy would surely be punished every time he would try to cross that

line, because now we had just pled the blood of Jesus over it, dedicated, anointed it as an embassy of Heaven so that Steve was an ambassador, is an ambassador of Christ, and that was his room. Even in my bedroom where I was on the phone with Kathy, there was just this light. It was flooded with light. Seeing something so real like that what the Lord was doing, doing something at that moment. And this encounter came when Kathy and I were praying.

What Marilyn didn't know was that ever since Steve's admittance to the ICU, I'd daily been praying for angels to be posted in his hospital room. Amazingly, as we prayed over the phone many days later, Marilyn saw those very angels there.

This was powerful and something the Lord knew I would need two days later.

Victories and Setbacks

When I got Steve's labs the morning of the seventeenth, I immediately texted a close friend of ours who is a pastor. He helped keep me steady in my faith throughout Steve's entire hospitalization and talked us through the ups and downs of Steve's condition, as things changed on a daily basis. He constantly reminded me that Jesus was right there with me and we were not alone, quoting Scripture like Hebrews 13:5: "He Himself has said 'I will never leave you nor forsake you.' So we may boldly say: 'The Lord is my helper; I will not fear. What can man do to me?'"

In the text, I told our pastor friend that Steve's oxygen requirement had increased to 100 percent (room air is 21 percent oxygen) and that his urine output was down. He promised to pray. Friends and family also promised to pray.

That day Steve developed kidney failure, making only one teaspoon of urine in twelve hours—dangerously low. I was sitting in Stacie's doctor's office when my phone rang and the pulmonologist told me her dad needed dialysis. They couldn't do it with him in a prone position, though. On top of that, Steve had also developed three blood clots, one in each leg and one in his arm, so they placed him on a potent blood thinner.

A level of discouragement hit me that's hard to describe, and I started to cry. But in one of the many moments of grace we were to experience, Stacie's doctor, who happens to be Steve's endocrinologist, saw my distress. She knows Steve well, and when she learned what was going on, she said, "Steve is incredibly healthy and strong, and there is absolutely no reason why he won't make a full recovery."

Her words were the shot of encouragement I needed, and I hung on every word she said. The Lord spoke through this doctor, and her positive attitude lifted me and Stacie in the moment and helped us press on, to continue the battle.

Then the pulmonologist decided to get a nephrology consultation. The nephrologist (kidney specialist) tried a Lasix drip to force Steve's kidneys to produce urine. The next morning, in my prayer room before the Father, praying harder than ever, I spent a long time praying in the Spirit. In a clear voice, the Lord said, *The Lasix drip will work.* His voice was in my spirit—not audible, but nevertheless clear. The Lord was showing me the nephrologist had the right idea, and it worked! Steve began to produce urine (and his kidney function improved dramatically over the next few weeks).

That morning I communicated to our pastor friend that Steve had remained stable overnight, his labs were good, and his kidneys were functioning. He responded with a passage that had been in his morning meditation: "I will bless the LORD who guides me; even at night my heart instructs me. I know the Lord is always with me. I will not be shaken, for he is right beside me" (Psalm 16:7–8 NLT).

To say Steve came close to dying is an undeniable truth. Even his primary care physician, Dr. Jeff, who stayed in daily contact with me and reviewed his hospital chart, gave Steve only a 15 to 20 percent chance of survival—though he didn't tell me this until later. Yet he was encouraging throughout.

When Steve got the tracheostomy, Dr. Jeff said he would have a "cool scar" someday.

When Steve had the gastrostomy, Dr. Jeff said he would have another "cool scar."

Well, Steve now has both "cool scars," and we are very glad they're just scars of things that were and are no more!

We—our family and our friends, whom we'll talk about later—warred in the supernatural. And after about a week on the ventilator, Steve improved greatly and was to be weaned off respiratory support.

Things were looking up.

Prayers were being answered.

And on December 23, Steve made a dramatic turnaround. The pulmonologist called to tell me she would wean his paralytic and sedation the next day and prepare for extubation. We were thrilled! I fell on my knees, praising God.

Then the unexpected happened.

The following morning, Steve's labs had deteriorated. His white blood cell count had jumped to twenty thousand, and he was not doing well. This turned out to be his first bacterial pneumonia. He had a total of three bacterial pneumonias caused by Pseudomonas, Acinetobacter, and Pseudomonas again. Consequently, Steve received three courses of antibiotics and remained on the ventilator for several more weeks—a total of an unbelievable forty-five days.

For part of that time, though, he was in Heaven. I just didn't know it.

3

The Heavenly Journey Begins

STEVE AND KATHY

He shall give His angels charge over you, to keep you in all
your ways.

Psalm 91:11

Steve

As intravenous sedatives took hold and medical personnel proceeded with intubation and connecting me to a ventilator, no
one knew that, for me, my eyes suddenly opened.

And someone was floating in front of me.

This "person's" head was about eighteen inches from my
face. He had an olive complexion and shoulder-length straight
brown hair parted in the middle. He wore a white robe with
gold trim around the sleeves and collar, and I could see the
handle of a sword in a sheath on his back. It was silver with
an inlaid design.

"Hi, Steve," he spoke gently. "My name is Marzuka. You spell that M-A-R-Z-U-K-A. I'm here to take you to Heaven for a short time while your body heals."

In that moment, both a calm and an excitement concerning what would happen next shot through me. God had sent an angel to take me to Heaven. Instantly, Psalm 91:11 came to mind: "He shall give His angels charge over you, to keep you in all your ways." And Hebrews 1:14 says, "What role then, do the angels have? The angels are spirit-messengers sent by God to serve those who are going to be saved" (TPT). Meeting my "spirit-messenger"—my guardian angel—was amazing and quite unexpected. And when he said he would be taking me to Heaven, I couldn't comprehend what that meant as I was connected to a ventilator.

"Okay," was all I could say, and it seemed like the natural response.

What took place next has forever changed me.

When I say "I" sat up, I mean my "spirit" sat up. My physical body remained in the bed, but my spirit, the real me, sat up. Your spirit is the real you—your innermost being. The soul is your mind, will, and emotions, which are all part of your inner being. The apostle Paul mentions this concept in 1 Thessalonians 5:23: "May your entire being—spirit, soul, and body—be kept completely flawless in the appearing of our Lord Jesus, the Anointed One" (TPT).

Marzuka turned around, and then we both traveled up toward the ceiling of that hospital room. In my peripheral vision, I could see some equipment and the door to the hallway on my left. To my right was a window, and I could tell it was daytime.

Marzuka and I traveled at great speed, passing through the ceiling as if it wasn't there. Soon we were up high in the sky.

Another second later, we were in outer space, moving so fast that the stars on either side of us seemed to streak by like millions of lights.

It was mind-blowing—nothing I could have ever dreamed would happen to me, a man who grew up going to a Baptist church. Sure, I heard the gospel from a young age, but the supernatural was never discussed there.

Before going on, let's step back into the past, first for me, then for Kathy.

Growing Up

As a child, I attended First Baptist Church with my mother, grandmother, brother, and sister. Our father was the only one who didn't attend regularly. My mother would say he was busy and had things to do. To his credit, he did attend church on Christmas, Easter, and special occasions, like when I was baptized. Surprisingly, though, his lack of church attendance didn't impact my walk with the Lord. When I was ten years old, I gave my heart to Him.

I'd been going to Sunday school since the fourth grade and was beginning to understand the plan of salvation when it dawned on me that I, too, needed Jesus. Our Sunday school teacher asked if anyone in the class wanted to give their life to the Lord, and several of us raised our hands. The teacher told us they would call us down to the front of the church during the main service.

During this altar call, I went down to the front and prayed to accept Jesus as my Savior. I felt excited—I had done the right thing. My mother and grandmother were happy about it as well. To my surprise, my Sunday school teacher gave me a copy of the Good News for Modern Man Bible. My brother, Ted, told me to start reading the book of John, so I did.

But by the time I was a junior in high school, I'd stopped going to church and had put God on the back burner, mostly due to the influence of friends who weren't serving the Lord. Later, the things one friend who was still in high school and I did were almost innocuous, but they were still small acts of sin that inched me further and further away from God, straying from Him gradually. Things like my writing notes for him to get out of school and signing his mother's name so we could hang out at the mall. Step by step, little by little, this behavior affected my faith.

The Voice That Saved My Life

Then I went to the University of Oklahoma (OU). One girl in particular and other friends pulled me in the wrong direction, and I didn't fight it. Drinking at bars, smoking—the trappings of the world drew me further and further into their grip. By the grace of God, there was no law breaking or issues with authorities or bosses, but I was running away from the path God had for me.

Still, He didn't forget about me.

During my sophomore year in college, I traveled home from OU for the weekend on a wintry night, but the roads were dry and there was no snow. It was about 11 p.m. when I left Norman in my trusty Vega, and I thought I was good to make the two-hour trek on the turnpike to Tulsa. I miscalculated how tired I was, though, and when I grew sleepy, for some bizarre reason I thought it would be all right to just shut my eyes for a little while.

I have no idea how long my eyes were closed, but suddenly, I heard an audible voice.

"Open your eyes and watch the road," the voice said. It was a male voice, speaking with authority, giving me a command.

I opened my eyes to find that my car had drifted onto the shoulder, heading toward a slope off the side of the road. Mildly startled, I calmly but quickly straightened the car back onto the road. Then after a pause, I looked around and checked the rearview mirror to see who'd spoken to me. But I was alone.

I continued, trying to put the strange voice out of my head.

Not long after, while still driving on the dark highway, my eyes became heavy again, and I closed them. This time I heard the same audible voice in a very stern tone:

"*Open* your eyes and *watch* the road!"

My eyes popped open, and I realized the car was careening toward a ditch. I quickly straightened it and again looked around to see who had spoken to me so emphatically.

I was still alone in the car.

My heart raced. My thoughts spun. What was going on?

Then out of the clear blue, it hit me: Was that God talking to me? There was no fear, there were no goose bumps, and there was no panic. I just wondered, *Am I hearing things? Or was that really God speaking?*

In the moment, nothing really changed in me. For sure, I didn't shut my eyes or feel sleepy for the rest of the trip, but I don't think I understood that God had saved my life.

Spiritual Turnaround

The whole experience, however, made me more God-conscious than I'd been—especially given the fact that I wasn't following Him. But my life really didn't change until I left college at OU after my sophomore year. I didn't know what I wanted to do with my life, so I moved back to Tulsa and worked at the research lab at Amoco while taking night classes at a local community college. It was there that I discovered what I would do as a profession—and rediscovered the love of Christ.

Working at Amoco, I became interested in computers as I ran data analysis for core samples, so I started taking programming classes at the community college and other general education classes. A girl I met at work invited me to go to church to hear a special speaker named Dave Roberson. I decided to go with her due to reevaluating my life and realizing my current friends had been leading me down the wrong path. The smoking, drinking, and going to bars was getting out of hand.

I also had a vivid memory from my days at OU. A friend's roommate got involved with some bad people. Then his drug addiction was out of control, he got himself into a bad situation one night, and he was killed by a gunshot to the head.

This was jarring. I realized I was being a hypocrite saying I was a Christian but not acting like one. I either needed to quit saying I was a Christian or change my ways. I decided my faith was more important than living a sinful lifestyle.

So when my friend invited me to the Roberson meeting, I went. When Mr. Roberson gave the altar call that night, I felt I was being offered a chance to get my life back on track. Rededicating myself to the Lord was the obvious choice, so I went down to the front, where someone prayed with me to do so. This decision added fuel to the desire to change my life.

A Faith Walk New to Me

Shortly after that experience, I started attending Victory Christian Center and made new friends through the Singles Bible

Fellowship group. This group taught me about the infilling of the Holy Spirit, which changed me from being the guy who sat in the back at church as an observer and a stranger to the gifts of the Spirit—especially the gift of tongues—to being actively involved in my faith church.

The defining moment was at Greg Ford's Bible Fellowship group on Friday nights. Having never heard about the gift of tongues or anyone praying in tongues as a kid, this was new to me. One week Greg taught about the Holy Spirit. Afterward, he said, "Would anyone here like to be filled with the Holy Spirit? Steve?"

And he looked right at me. I didn't say anything, so he asked me if I'd like to have hands laid on me to be filled with the Holy Spirit. I must have said yes, because the next thing I knew about ten people were laying their hands on me and praying in tongues. I wasn't sure how to respond. However, I soon found myself speaking in tongues as well. I had a bunch of questions, though, like "How can I find out what I was saying?" Greg said to pray for an interpretation.

I was a Baptist boy having a Pentecostal experience. But I learned that the Holy Spirit guides us and will show us things when we pray. He gives us direction. I also began learning about our authority in Christ. All these ideas were new to me.

What solidified my walk was a new group of friends, people I could attend church services with on Sunday mornings and evenings and on Wednesday evenings. This is where I met people like Steve and Marilyn and Mary, who became lifelong friends and were backbones during my battle to stay alive and the recovery process.

It's also where I met the love of my life.

Meeting My Future Wife

It was a Friday night Singles Bible Fellowship in 1987 and Kathy's first time to attend. She seemed shy and quiet, but she had a beautiful smile and I was very attracted to her. After the Bible study, we both went out to a late-night restaurant for casual fellowship with other members of the group. I learned that Kathy was in her third year of medical school and had recently experienced a broken engagement. She had a clerkship in Surgery and Internal Medicine that fall and worked a lot of hours, all while studying as much as possible. Kathy's only interest at the time was doing God's will and becoming a doctor. There was no room for a romantic relationship in her life.

Since she wasn't eager to date again, I decided to spend time getting to know her in our group setting. I'll let Kathy tell you a little bit more about that before I go on with my story.

Kathy

When I was in my second year of medical school, I got engaged. Unfortunately, I wasn't listening to the voice of the Holy Spirit. The Lord had told me to end the relationship, but I allowed my natural mind to take over, and I reasoned that I didn't want to be the cause of pain for my boyfriend. Besides, I enjoyed his company and wanted to continue the relationship, so I accepted his proposal. We were engaged in September 1986 and planned to marry in June 1987.

My mother and I planned a big Italian wedding for the week after I was to take the first part of my NBME (National Board of Medical Examiners) exam. This is the hardest of the three board exams as it covers all the basic science of the first two years of medical school. As the end of the year and the exam approached, I was excited about the wedding. I had the gown and was ready to order invitations. The reception was planned, and my mother had put deposits on everything.

Then one day in April—when I would soon be taking my semester exams, finals, and boards—my fiancé suddenly told me he no longer wanted to marry me. He broke our engagement over the phone, and I was devastated. He gave no explanation at all.

Extreme depression set in. I would sit in the back of a class and cry instead of taking in the lecture. I cried constantly, and for the first few weeks, I was barely functional. I couldn't concentrate. Any studying I attempted was unproductive.

Part of the pain was a result of knowing the Lord had told me to break off this relationship over a year before and I hadn't obeyed Him. I entered a time of needing healing for my emotions and forgiveness for my disobedience. I continued crying every evening for the first few months after the breakup. Then as time passed, I would just cry on Friday and Saturday nights—times that brought memories of dating my fiancé.

Fighting Back from Depression

I lived at home during medical school, and one day my mother finally said, "Go out and do something on the weekends. You've got to stop crying all the time."

Her advice was enough of a jolt to get me slowly moving forward. I met a girl at church named Hope who hosted a singles Bible Fellowship group on Friday nights. This seemed to be a good place to make new friends—all my old friends had ties to my former fiancé.

I remember the first time I went to Hope's apartment for a meeting, and I'll never forget what she whispered in my ear when I arrived: "You're a brave girl."

I didn't feel brave. On the contrary, I felt timid and incredibly awkward.

After the study, several of us went to a late-night restaurant for food and fellowship. Joel, one of the guys I'd met, was joking around and made me laugh. God knew I needed to laugh. I'm naturally a very serious person and quite an introvert. As I laughed with my new friends that night, I felt a burst of joy inside me. I realized I hadn't laughed in months, and it was a welcome feeling.

Proverbs 17:22 says, "A merry heart does good, like medicine, but a broken spirit dries the bones." I had had enough of the bone-drying, broken-spirit experience. I was ready for a merry heart.

It's amazing how our Father designed our bodies to release enkephalins and endorphins when we laugh. These hormones have such positive effects on our immune system and our overall health. My undergraduate senior paper was in pharmacology, studying the effects of stress on the immune system. My research with laboratory mice demonstrated that stress suppresses the immune system, allowing damaging effects to occur in our cells. On the contrary, feelings of joy strengthen our immune response. Our immune system is responsible for many aspects of surveillance in our bodies. It protects us from invasion by infectious agents and, when working as God intended, seeks out and destroys abnormal cell growths that lead to tumors and cancers.

The laughter that night and many nights that followed were driving out the depression in my soul and healing my body at the same time.

Dating Ups and Downs with Steve

Three guys named Steve were there that night, and Steve Boyls was one of them. He had large glasses, a mustache, and a big smile. And he seemed like someone I'd like to have as a friend. Steve and I did quickly become friends, and in sharing my recent experiences with him, I found him to be kind and understanding. He never pushed, but in a short time he indicated that he wanted to pursue a relationship beyond friendship. Wanting to spend more time with me, at times he would say we were going to a group activity, but then we'd be the only ones who showed up at the venue. I would ask where everyone else was, and when Steve told me again and again that they couldn't make it, I suspected what he was doing: He conveniently forgot to invite our other friends.

I fell for him, we started dating, and over the next three years we dated on and off. I was quite reluctant to put my emotions at risk again.

Due to the demands of medical school, many times our evenings together were spent studying in the medical library. Steve was a full-time student in computer science at that time.

We both graduated in 1989, Steve from the University of Tulsa and me from Oral Roberts University Medical School. I had chosen to do my residency in Pediatrics in St. Louis, Missouri, and the night before I moved, I broke up with Steve for the third time. We had just packed the rented truck to leave for St. Louis in the morning, and he was going to help me move by driving the truck with our friend, Joel. I told Steve I just wanted to be friends.

Then after he left that night, I realized he might not show up the next morning to help me move. What a stupid thing I'd done! Yet to describe Steve as persistent and patient is an understatement. He's told me the Lord spoke to him about being patient with me as I had been hurt in the past, and his actions the next day proved his obedience. To my amazement, bright and early the next morning both Steve and Joel arrived to help me move. I was floored, truly. When Steve and I said our goodbyes in St. Louis, I didn't think I'd hear from him again. But his obedience and belief in the Lord's word to him shone through once more.

Three weeks later he asked if he could visit. I said yes, thinking it was just as friends. He came to St. Louis and we went out to lunch, but I still didn't want to get back together. When he returned to Tulsa, he called me a few more times and talked me into giving him another chance. I finally agreed, and we started a long-distance relationship. This was expensive as long-distance phone calls cost about 25 cents per minute back then. Every month we each had a $100 phone bill—an astronomical price at the time. Steve's mother worked for Southwestern Bell at the time and helped him pay some of the bills.

But I still wasn't ready to totally commit. In fact, I tried to break up with Steve a fourth time. As I was talking, he laughed. I was shocked at his response, but then I realized how funny it was, and I laughed too. The joy I felt convinced me to accept his love for me.

The Gift of Marriage

Steve and I saw each other about once a month when I had two days off in a row and got a cheap flight to Tulsa on TWA.

We got engaged in September 1990. I was in my second year of residency in St. Louis, and since Steve had a job in Tulsa, I worked to transfer to a Tulsa pediatric program to complete the third year of my residency. The transfer happened, and we married on June 29, 1991. It was the happiest day of my life, and the beginning of a life of wonder and pain, of love and struggle, of growing and deepening our walks with Christ and each other. And it set us on course for what was to come.

Looking back, I think, *How could I resist such love?* It reminds me of the love the Father has for us. Jesus tells us that He goes after the lost sheep. He doesn't just wait for them to come to Him; He's proactive. Steve never gave up on me despite my best efforts to discourage him. That is a characteristic of love: "Love never gives up, never loses faith, is always hopeful, and endures through every circumstance" (1 Corinthians 13:7 NLT).

Little did I know that decades later I would be the one who never gave up on Steve when he was dying in the ICU. I'll let him resume the story.

Steve

Just as quickly as Marzuka and I passed through space, I realized I was in a grassy field walking toward a building with him. Imagine, just a moment earlier I was incredibly sick, on a ventilator in the ICU. Now I felt totally healthy. My physical body was still in that hospital room, but my spirit was in a place of unspeakable beauty. Second Corinthians 5:8–9 says, "Yes, we are fully confident, and we would rather be away from these earthly bodies, for then we will be at home with the Lord. So whether we are here in this body or away from this body, our goal is to please him" (NLT).

Then I noticed I was no longer wearing a hospital gown. Instead, I wore a short-sleeved white robe with gold trim on the sleeves, collar, and hem. The trim was about one and a half inches wide and had a square pattern. I had a red sash around my waist, and the robe came down to my ankles. I was also wearing comfortable sandals. I felt younger and noticed there was no pain at all in my body.

The Welcome Center

As Marzuka and I stepped inside the building, a man behind a counter on the other side of a white archway spoke up. "Hello, Steve!" he called out. "Welcome to Heaven!"

I walked through the archway behind Marzuka, and instinctively I knew this was Heaven's Welcome Center. There's no theological reason why God would have a Welcome Center in Heaven. However, several Scriptures refer to welcoming people into the kingdom of God. And Jesus mentioned welcoming little children: "Anyone who welcomes a little child like this on my behalf welcomes me, and anyone who welcomes me welcomes not only me but also my Father who sent me" (Mark 9:37 NLT). The apostle Paul, speaking of Epaphroditus, asked the Philippian church to welcome him: "Welcome him in the Lord's love and with great joy, and give him the honor that people like him deserve" (Philippians 2:29 NLT).

Jesus Himself welcomes His sheep to inherit His kingdom in Matthew 25:34 (NLT): "Come, you who are blessed by my Father, inherit the Kingdom prepared for you from the creation of the world." And our Creator God welcomes each one of us to receive His life and love through Jesus Christ: "God so loved the world that He gave His only begotten Son, that whoever believes in Him should not perish but have everlasting life" (John 3:16).

Jesus said, "In my Father's house are many mansions; if it were not so, I would have told you. I go to prepare a place for you" (John 14:2). And He's also prepared this Welcome Center to introduce us to that blessed place. While there, I remembered stopping at state welcome centers on family driving vacations. These centers provide information about the state you've entered and often have hospitality desks, all to say, "We're glad you're here. We hope you enjoy your visit." Earth is a reflection of Heaven. We have Welcome Centers here; why not expect Heaven to have one?

The Welcome Center resembled a fancy hotel check-in desk, but none I've seen can compare given the ornate decorations I encountered. The ceiling was at least twenty feet high, and the floor was crystal clear and shone brilliantly. The counter was curved with a wooden countertop and wood carvings on the front. Above the counter was a large chandelier, about six feet in diameter and five feet tall. It was gold and held a myriad of gemstones giving off light—glistening diamonds, each as large as a softball, and rubies, garnets, emeralds, and sapphires.

The walls of the Welcome Center had four carvings of various scenes, and later I learned that each one was a scene from Heaven with some significance for me.

The first carving was a relief of a beautiful meadow full of vibrant lush grass and many flowers in perfectly manicured flowerbeds. It was a serene landscape.

The second was a mountain scene with tall and majestic peaks. It looked like there was no snow on the mountaintops, but I could see trails leading through the passes and valleys.

This stirred memories of when Kathy and I and our daughters lived in Colorado, near the base of Pikes Peak. In fact, our younger daughter was born in Colorado. I'm familiar with living near mountains and enjoying their beauty.

The next scene was a V-shaped valley. This valley was full of lush grass, an abundance of flowers, and many trees on the slopes.

The final scene was a beach with palm trees in small groves, which looked similar to the royal palms we have on Earth.

"The Things You Need to See"

The man behind the counter looked to be in his mid to late twenties. He stood about six feet tall and also wore a white robe. Now he smiled and said to me, "Marzuka will be your guide, and he'll show you the things you need to see." (Later Marzuka told me, "There are many wonderful things to see here, and it will take an eternity to see them all. The Lord continues to create in Heaven, and it's amazing to see His creation.")

"Okay," I said again, not knowing how else to respond.

What else could I say? I was still trying to process where I was and what I was experiencing. There are no words to describe the beauty one encounters just at the edge or entrance of Heaven. It's more than anyone can tell or even imagine.

4

Family, Friends
—and Pets Too!

STEVE

God will wipe away every tear from their eyes; there shall be
no more death, nor sorrow, nor crying. There shall be no more
pain, for the former things have passed away.

Revelation 21:4

Marzuka and I moved on through the Welcome Center, then
exited, turned to our left, and walked down a golden street that
was pure and crystal clear. On one side was a large, beautiful
meadow, and I followed Marzuka into it. I was staggered again
by the immensity and beauty of what I saw and felt.

As we walked, Marzuka told me we were going to see people
special to me. I heard him, but I was taken in by the grass and
flowers, which were lush and full of life. In fact, when I stepped

on the grass, the blades sprang back up! The flowers had many colors on each petal, and their sweet fragrance flooded my senses. Giant trees with low-hanging, curved branches filled the area, and birds chirped in the trees. When I finally looked straight ahead, pulling my gaze from all the scenery enveloping me, I saw movement in the distance.

Meeting My Dogs

Suddenly, I was surrounded by eight dogs, and I knew them all: Thor, Yaz, Brooks, Pete, Louie, Papi, Sam, and Jenna. These were my dogs over the years, and they'd all died.

I adopted Thor before I married; he was half Chow and half Labrador, a formidable sight. Now he was pretty playful and looked like he enjoyed being with the pack.

Yaz, Brooks, and Pete were the huskies Kathy and I adopted after we got married. They died from various causes at about twelve to fourteen years old. Now they were strong, energetic, and friendly as ever.

Louie we lost as a puppy when he got out of the yard and never returned despite our best efforts to find him. In Heaven, he was now full-grown and beautiful.

Papi was a Great Pyrenees mix who chose us one hot summer day when he walked into our garage. Papi had only one eye and limped, and Kathy always joked that we were his retirement home. In the meadow, Papi had both eyes and could run and jump just like the rest—no limp!

Sam and Jenna were siblings we'd adopted as puppies and had passed a year and a half before my trip to Heaven. Both had tumors that affected their ability to walk and, eventually, stand. But right in front of my eyes, they were perfect, running and playing!

Of course, the dogs all wanted my attention, and I took the time to pet each one. Emotions overwhelmed me, and I couldn't wait to tell Kathy, "Our pets do go to Heaven." God cares about all that concerns us, even our pets. The Bible tells us He even cares about the sparrows: "Not a single sparrow can fall to the ground without your Father knowing it" (Matthew 10:29 NLT). The Lord knew our dogs were important to me and knows I'll enjoy spending eternity with them close by.

While petting the dogs, I saw an angel flying in the sky about two to three hundred feet away from me. It was too far away for me to see much detail, but I knew it was an angel. I tried my best to notice everything in my surroundings. However, I remained overwhelmed by the dogs, the grass, the flowers, and the trees.

Meeting My Friend Gary

The dogs ran off through the meadow as a pack, and I encountered my first human as Marzuka and I explored the meadow. It was my friend Gary, a fellow believer and coworker, who'd passed away more than ten years earlier. A forgiving person, he didn't have a mean bone in his body. Several people had taken advantage of him while I knew him, but he never said a bad word about anyone. He was always fun to talk to at work, and now we enjoyed our conversation in Heaven.

I was stunned at how he looked. Gary had struggled with his weight, but in Heaven, he was trim and healthy.

"How do you like it here?" I asked him. Kathy chuckled when I told her that was the first thing I asked, but I was at a loss for words.

"It's great!" he exclaimed. "I can eat whatever I want!"

We talked about food and the wonders I was taking in. Eventually, he walked into the meadow, and I found a family member waiting for me: my niece, Beth.

Meeting My Niece and Brother

Beth had passed away in the 1990s, killed in a car accident one week before her wedding. She was so excited to see me, and her face glowed with the presence of God. Her long, thick, flowing brown hair contrasted with her white robe. As we talked, she said she often saw her dad in Heaven and hoped I'd get to see him. He was my brother.

My heart jumped. Ted had also died in a car accident, about six months after Kathy and I were married.

After my conversation with Beth, we parted ways, and Marzuka and I turned in a different direction. As we walked, I saw Ted about fifteen feet away. We grabbed each other and hugged.

"Ted, it's so good to see you!" I told him.

"I'm so glad to see you too," he said. "But"—he looked at me intently—"I know you'll be going back soon."

Ted told me he attends the apostle Paul's Bible studies and goes to baseball games in Heaven. I found this quite interesting and wondered if I could experience some of these things with him. This was a dream come true. After Kathy and I married, I missed out on the chance to gain wisdom about married life from Ted and learn from his years of experience. I missed him so much in part because he passed away so unexpectedly. Now I had so many emotions building up inside of me. I was overwhelmed with joy to see my precious brother. God is so gracious!

"Ted, it's been almost thirty years," I said. "I've missed you."

He paused and stared at me, a look of surprise on his face. "It feels like I just got here," he responded. "Wow."

Before long I found myself leaving the meadow with Marzuka and walking down a street made of some beautiful transparent material. I sensed it was gold, but it was beyond description. At the same time, I heard beautiful voices unlike any I'd heard before, singing praise to God. Although I couldn't see anyone, this beautiful music filled the air.

"This is one of many heavenly choirs that sing praise to God," Marzuka said.

Almost instantly, I understood that the choirs take turns singing to the Lord. He mentioned my mom and grandmother were singing in the same choir, the one I could hear. Strange—I didn't detect one bad note from those singing. I was amazed at how wonderful they sounded, especially since my mother and grandmother weren't known for their singing ability on Earth.

Now walking down a clear, pure gold street, I noticed the buildings on either side of the road had unfamiliar architectural details. Many corners were curved and ornate unlike the stick-built structures we have here. Just ahead of us, passing the buildings, were two angelic beings, quite tall and well-built. Both wore long-sleeved white robes with gold trim, and they each had a sword in a sheath across their backs.

Meeting Kathy's Parents

As I turned my attention from the beautiful architecture to the road in front of me, I saw Kathy's parents walking toward us, and joy flooded me. Manny and Eileen both loved Christ, and I was excited to see them. They were happy to see me as well, and I wondered if they'd been expecting me. They stopped to talk, and I hugged them both.

Marzuka said, "He's just here for a short time, and he'll be returning soon."

Eileen told me Heaven is wonderful and her mansion is beautiful. She also said she'd met Kenneth Hagin and talked to him for a while.

I was struck by how young they both looked, having never seen them in their earlier years. Manny, a Filipino, had thick black hair. And they were both healthy and full of energy. I was shocked by how different their physical condition was. Manny had battled brain cancer, miraculously living for five years after the oncologist initially gave him only six months. He'd fought through brain surgery and whole-brain radiation to shrink the tumor and had mentally and physically deteriorated, graduating to Heaven in 2009.

Eileen had lost most of her vision and was hospitalized in the ICU with pneumonia when she passed. This was at the end of nine years of depression and oppression after her husband died. She missed Manny so much and never got over her grief.

Now they stood in front of me, smiling, happy, and enjoying the wonders of Heaven.

"Tell Kathy I love her," she said.

"I love her too," Manny added.

We parted, and oddly, I did not feel sorrow. I was happy that I could see them, and I can attest to the fact that there is no sadness in Heaven. Whether I was leaving Kathy's parents, my brother, or those I would soon meet, I never felt a sense of loss even though I knew I was there temporarily. In the time ahead, I would learn a concept difficult to explain: In Heaven, there are no negative feelings—only joy.

Meeting My Parents

Farther down the street as we passed others traveling on it, two more people walked toward me. It took a heartbeat to recognize my parents because they seemed to be in their twenties, but I did and threw my arms around them. My mother had shoulder-length brown hair. My father had a full head of hair, fuller than I think I'd ever seen it. He looked fabulous. They both wore white robes like others I'd seen and red sashes around their waists. A gold pattern was embroidered on the robes' sleeves and hems.

Mom moved to Heaven in 2010, having had a lung disease called pulmonary fibrosis. Just before she died, she insisted that a man was standing by her hospital room door. I couldn't see anyone there. Later, after we'd left her hospital room, she told the nurse several people were in the room and asked who they were. The nurse told her she didn't see anyone, but Mom knew what she saw. I now understand the "people" were angels who escorted her to her new home in Heaven.

Mom told me she sang with my grandmother in a choir. Marzuka had told me that, but now I found it even more surprising; I'd had no idea my mother could sing. *Are hidden talents revealed in the heavenly realm?* I wondered.

Dad passed away in 2002 after dealing with heart problems and bladder cancer, and I'd wondered about his relationship with the Lord. He told me he was grateful to all those who prayed for him and told him about Jesus.

"Even though it may have seemed there was no difference," he said, "there was a change on the inside."

Never give up on your family members who need Jesus. Invest your time in prayer for them and expect a great return—their return to the Lord. It's the greatest return on investment ever!

I told my parents I'd seen Ted and Beth.

"We see them often," they said.

Sometime later during my time in Heaven, I visited both my parents' homes.

My dad's mansion

In my father's mansion, I found myself in his "carving room." Dad had been a woodcarver in his spare time and spent more time carving after he retired. The room was about thirty feet by forty feet and had high ceilings with large windows. The walls were white, and the floor was a crystal-clear material. From the windows, I could see other mansions in the distance. There were large trees outside, as well as plush grass.

In the room were many pedestals with wood carvings on them. On Earth, Dad had won contests with his relief work in wood carving. Now he had so many pieces on display.

"These are beautiful," I said.

"I've worked long and hard on each one of them," he told me with no sign of frustration or tiredness. (Everyone I encountered looked youthful and energetic.)

In the middle of the room was a pedestal with his current project—a wooden cube carved with elaborate designs. My father said he was experimenting with new ideas for carving.

"If I make a mistake," he said, "all I have to do is speak a word, and it corrects."

I was stunned.

"However," he went on, "I prefer to do it correctly rather than use my words to fix it."

Mark 11:23 sprang to remembrance: "I say to you, whoever says to this mountain, 'Be removed and be cast into the sea,' and does not doubt in his heart, but believes that those things he says will be done, he will have whatever he says."

God takes our words seriously, and there's tremendous power in the words we speak. Proverbs 18:21 says, "Death and life are in the power of the tongue." Your words are important. When they agree with what you believe in your heart, your words will come to pass (Mark 11:23). This is such an important truth. We should weigh our words carefully and not allow our enemy, the devil, to influence what we say.

But when we do make a mistake, we can repent and ask God to forgive us for idle words, angry words, foolish words, and any words that are not pleasing to Him. Pray and believe for a harvest on all the words of life you speak. Speaking God's Word, the Holy Scriptures, is the best way to receive blessing from Heaven. In Heaven, the spoken word comes to pass immediately. Jesus taught us to pray "on earth, as it is in heaven" (Matthew 6:10).

As we looked at my father's most recent carving, he started to talk about Kathy. "You are fortunate to be married to such a good wife," he said. "She's taking outstanding care of you down there."

I understood what he meant: My physical body was still alive in the ICU and attached to a ventilator, while my spirit—the real me, the inner man—was visiting Heaven. He never said directly that those in Heaven can watch us, yet somehow he knew what was going on in the hospital. Later, after I returned to my body, I was overcome by the amount of care Kathy had shown me.

It's incredible what insights I've had since seeing things from Heaven's perspective. Heaven sees everything through the finished work of Christ. There's never any question or doubt about who the Victor is. Colossians 2:15 tells us, "Jesus made a public spectacle of all the powers and principalities of darkness, stripping away from them every weapon and all their spiritual authority and power to accuse us. And by the power of the cross, Jesus led them around as prisoners in a procession of triumph" (TPT).

We should face every difficult circumstance of life knowing that Jesus has made us more than conquerors: "Yet even in the midst of all these things, we triumph over them all, for God has made us to be more than conquerors, and his demonstrated love is our glorious victory over everything!" (Romans 8:37 TPT).

My mother's mansion

My mother's mansion is a two-story home with a second-floor balcony that spans the width of the house. The outside is a glossy, very light pink, a favorite color of hers, and many colorful flowers and trees adorn her front yard.

As I approached the decorative silver gate to her home, Marzuka motioned for me to go in while he waited outside. The arched entryway opened into a lovely foyer with a high arched ceiling. On the right, I noticed a carved hall table with a vase of flowers. Just ahead was a great room and a stairway. I entered and ascended the stairs to a room that reminded me of a kitchen, although I didn't see any appliances. There at a dining table sat my mother and grandmother, who beckoned me to have a seat. The chairs were cushioned and comfortable. Mom said she had something good for me to eat. She left momentarily and returned with a delicious cake that resembled a pineapple upside-down cake. We all ate the cake and enjoyed each other's company.

Before leaving Mom's house, I gave her and Grandma hugs and said my goodbyes. But there was no sorrow in our embrace—only joy that I'd had the opportunity to see them. I knew I would see them again.

Now, before parting at our initial meeting, my mother asked about my daughters. We spoke briefly about the girls, and my parents smiled as if they already knew details about them.

After we left Mom and Dad on that heavenly street, Marzuka and I came to a grassy field near a large baseball stadium. There I encountered something truly amazing: a little boy I didn't recognize but who knew me.

It rocked my world.

5

A Firm Faith
and God's Grace

KATHY

Now faith is the substance of things hoped for, the evidence of things not seen.

Hebrews 11:1

While Steve traveled to the most wondrous place, Christmas 2021 was not a holiday for me and the rest of our family. There were no decorations or celebrations. There were no parties or gifts. The house was too quiet—Steve's laughter was gone, and so was a lot of the joy.

Since by the hospital's count we were still under twenty days since he'd contracted COVID, Steve remained in isolation. But I received the best gift I could: I was allowed a brief visit with him. And because it was Christmas, two people could be in his room at a time.

I stayed with Steve the whole visit while my daughter Stephanie and Janie took turns coming in. We had to wear N95 masks and gowns and gloves, and Janie said it was like suiting up to go into a hazmat area. It was a short visit, but I was able to talk to Steve even though he couldn't respond, hold his hand in my gloved ones, and pray for him.

It was nice to see him for all of us. We'd been texting with Steve one day, and then the next day he was intubated and sedated and we couldn't talk with him. It had been jarring.

A Snowstorm, Plumbing Problem, and More

After the Christmas visit, a snowstorm hit Oklahoma. At one point, we lost power, and Steve's computers all shut down. Since I'm not computer savvy, I left them alone, praying they'd still work when he got home. And with the power out, I couldn't get the garage door open, so my car was stuck in the garage. I called Janie and asked her to take me to work. She picked me up and took me there, and then Stacie picked me up later in the day.

Once the days started to warm a touch, we developed a leak when a water pipe burst in our front yard. We called a plumber, and he dug a six-foot hole and made repairs, costing a small fortune. At the time, our financial situation wasn't good. This expense with the plumber added to the burden of having lost a great deal of money in a business situation shortly before Steve got sick and losing income with him in the hospital.

All this was overwhelming. At one point, I messaged Marilyn, asking her what God was showing her about the situation. She said, "What I heard from the Lord is it's not your fault, so quit it. That's not right. We're praying for mercy healing now. He's got to keep fighting and he's got a decree."

Continuing My New Routine

I still followed Steve's labs every day: complete blood counts (CBC), inflammatory markers (CRP), electrolytes (sodium, potassium, chloride, carbon dioxide), and kidney function (creatinine and BUN). I'd also find out what his ventilator settings were, what percent of oxygen he was receiving, what his oxygen saturation was through the night, and whether they did a blood gas test. In addition, I wanted to know if anything else happened through the night. Then I'd text the information to a group of doctor girlfriends, as well as many others who were praying for Steve.

After Christmas, the hospital took Steve out of isolation, and we were allowed to visit him more regularly. On one of the first days, his blood pressure was elevated and quite unstable. The hospitalist thought he'd had a stroke and sent him—ventilator and all—to radiology for a CT scan of his head. Thank God, it was normal.

Some days I would have to make my own morning rounds before I could visit Steve. Then I'd get to his room in time to spend about forty-five minutes before I had to leave for the office. During that time, I'd evaluate everything I saw and talk to the nurses and respiratory therapists who were available.

At noon, I'd rush back to the hospital to check on Steve and hope I could catch the attending physician, a hospitalist or pulmonologist, making rounds. Then I would go back to the office for the afternoon.

After work I went directly to the hospital and stayed with Steve until between 10 p.m. and midnight, depending on how he was doing. I'd go home to sleep for a few hours and then start the process again. On the weekends, I spent most of the day at the hospital with Steve.

Here again, Marilyn would step in when I needed it and tell me, "Okay, Kathy, you go to sleep now. I'm awake. I'll be praying. I'll be praying as I do my business around here. You get some sleep; you need rest."

The hospital rule was that only two people could visit on any given day. Since Stacie was in school all day and Janie was retired, most days the other person visiting was Janie.

A Blessing Named Stacie

Stacie helped me keep the household going, took care of the dogs, and most of the time, she made her own meals. She was a tremendous help to me during this time, which she describes this way:

> As a senior in high school, I was doing regular senior activities. I had a part-time job as an opener at Starbucks. I would come home and take care of my dogs, and I basically kept the house clean. My mom was pretty much spending all of her time either at the hospital or at work, and so at home it was just me. I was buying my own groceries at that point. I was pretty much completely self-sufficient. I was trying to get auditions ready for school, and I was applying for college. Instead of being aided in the process by my parents being there, I kind of had to do all of that by myself.

We had two dogs: Boomer, a ten-year-old Great Pyrenees whom we'd rescued, and Winnie, a husky puppy who was less than a year old. This combination was quite challenging even when everyone was well and at home. It was even more difficult in our situation. Boomer would wander the house, looking for Steve. Every night and morning, he would just stare at Steve's side of the bed. He became noticeably depressed. However, he developed a new love for Stacie and really began to seek her out for attention. Winnie was her usual hyperactive self. Steve says he's still trying to find her "off switch" but to no avail.

Looking back, I can say that my faith was firm, and I refused to accept defeat and death while Steve suffered in the hospital. This was because of the grace of God and the foundation of faith firmly rooted in me from my childhood. I want to tell you more about how that foundation was built in my life early on, because it's an important part of what got me through the ordeal I faced later while Steve was in Heaven. See a coming chapter for that story, but meanwhile, let's get back to Steve as he relates one of the most amazing parts of his experience in Heaven—a meeting that profoundly affected us both.

6

"I Think You're My Dad"

STEVE AND KATHY

For You formed my inward parts; you covered me in
   my mother's womb. I will praise
You, for I am fearfully and wonderfully made;
   marvelous are Your works, and that
my soul knows very well.

Psalm 139:13–14

Steve

In 2002, before we had our younger daughter, Stacie, Kathy had
a miscarriage. She'd come up positive on a home pregnancy test,
but things weren't right in the fourth week. It was at Thanksgiving, and she didn't feel well and had excessive bleeding. As
our six-year-old daughter Stephanie and I put up the Christmas

tree, Kathy lay on the couch, trying to enjoy the holiday but aware she was probably losing the baby.

When she went to the obstetrician the following week, they couldn't find a pregnancy on ultrasound. She had a difficult time with the loss of this baby and went through a grieving period years later. She always felt that it was a boy and named him Daniel.

Looking across this grassy field where Marzuka and I were walking, I saw a little boy, about five or six years old, coming toward us. He was wearing a white robe with a red sash and sandals. He didn't run; he just walked up to me.

He said, "I think you're my dad. My name is Daniel."

I cannot express to you my shock and amazement at those words. As I stood looking at the boy, I could see Kathy and I blended in his appearance. He had brown eyes, skin olive in color, and brown hair, all like Kathy's. His hair was wavy like mine. It was parted on the side, combed across with bangs, and it hung over his ears slightly and down to his neck. I noticed his nose was like mine, as were many of his facial features. How I wished Kathy could have been there to meet him!

So many questions flooded my mind. Why was he still so small? I've heard that children grow slowly in Heaven so their parents can help raise them when they join them in their heavenly home.

As I looked into this little boy's big eyes, saw his beautiful smile, and admired his floppy hair, I knew he was my child.

"Well, my wife and I lost a baby many years ago before he could be born," I said. "We were going to name him Daniel."

Daniel told me he was very small when he arrived in Heaven and was raised in a special place for babies. Then before I knew it, he grabbed my legs and gave me a big hug. I leaned over and hugged him back, overcome with emotion once again. If there were crying in Heaven, I would have cried at that moment. I was thrilled to see him, yet I wished I could have spent the last twenty years with him. For now, it's enough that I will be spending eternity with my little boy, Daniel.

"Your mom would be so happy that I met you," I said. "She's very pretty."

"I know she is. I can't wait to see her someday," Daniel replied.

It struck me that, like my parents, Kathy's parents, my brother, and my niece, Daniel came and found me. Like the others, he seemed to know I was visiting Heaven and was eager to meet me. My son knew who I was and what his mother looked like too.

Daniel and I played catch for a while in that grassy field. The ball we used just seemed to appear—I have no idea where it came from. I was stunned at how well he could throw the ball; this "young" boy had such a good throwing arm.

I've always loved baseball, and I've been an avid Red Sox fan most of my life. My brother taught me how to play baseball, and as kids we spent many hours practicing with the whiffle ball and bat. Back and forth, Daniel and I whipped the ball around. There was so much joy in the moment that I can't relate it in words. I felt such pride at the strength of his arm, and I didn't want the moment to end.

God's Love and Grace

Of all my experiences in Heaven, meeting Daniel is the one that touches my wife the most. I didn't begin to remember my heavenly journey until weeks later, after my hospitalizations, but when I did and told Kathy about Daniel, she started to cry. Now every time she thinks of him, she weeps. Can you imagine the grace and mercy of our Father God that He allowed me to see my child in Heaven—the one who was never born on this earth?

If you've ever lost a baby, know that your child is in Heaven waiting for you—praise God! He takes special care of these little ones, and this blessed hope is truly for everyone. If you know Jesus, you will be reunited with your baby. There is no sorrow there, and all is forgiven, even if your loss is from abortion. Your child will find you in Heaven and be thrilled to see you! And your child is watching you as well.

God is the originator of the family. He created us because He wanted a family. When sin separated us from Him, He loved us enough to send His Son Jesus to become the sacrificial Lamb who would take away our sin and give us a way back to our Father God. He knows how important our children are to us. It thrills the heart of God to reunite parents with their children, whether in Heaven or here.

After my encounter with Daniel, I found myself inside a baseball stadium. I'll tell you more about that in the next chapter, but first I want Kathy to tell you what's on her heart about Daniel.

Kathy

I was thirty-nine when we decided to try to have another child. My pregnancy with Stephanie had been a rough one. I vomited many times daily for four months straight, then had one "good" month, then went into pre-term labor and had to be in the hospital for one week and on bed rest the remainder of my pregnancy. I was miserable. It took me a long time to be willing to go through that again. But I got pregnant quickly after I stopped taking birth control pills, and I was excited since the obstetrician had told me it might take a while.

I was only about four to five weeks pregnant when I miscarried. I was devastated. However, only a few months later I was pregnant with Stacie, and my grief turned to joy with the arrival of our new little girl. God was merciful, and the loss of Daniel also didn't have a big impact on our marriage. But Stephanie had been hoping for a sibling for a while, and years later she told me she was heartbroken.

Grief Delayed

I didn't grieve completely until years later, triggered by a death in my family. When my father died in April 2009, I attended a grief recovery class with my mother. The counselor said we could go through the grieving process for whatever loss affected us the most. Although I missed my dad a great deal, I didn't feel the overwhelming grief I realized I felt for the baby I lost. In my heart I felt it had been a boy, and I'd named him after my favorite Old Testament Bible character—Daniel.

I went through the class and did all the exercises as I was grieving for Daniel, but I never told my mother I did it for my son, not my father.

I Learn About Daniel

I well remember the moment Steve told me about Daniel in Heaven. I laughed, I cried, I asked a ton of questions. What color were his eyes, his hair? Was his hair straight or curly? How old did he appear? What was he wearing? How tall was he? Did he live with one of my parents or Steve's parents? Why did he still seem so young? Of course, Steve didn't know the answers to all my questions, but he could describe Daniel's appearance and mannerisms.

I so yearn to see my son who is in Heaven! Every time Steve talks about Daniel, my eyes fill with tears and I'm overcome. And knowing about him has drawn Steve and me closer as we both now have this amazing hope that we'll spend eternity in Heaven with our precious son.

7

Baseball in Heaven, Prayers on Earth

STEVE AND KATHY

Eye has not seen, nor ear heard, nor have entered into the heart of man the things which God has prepared for those who love Him. But God has revealed them to us through His Spirit. For the Spirit searches all things, yes, the deep things of God.

1 Corinthians 2:9–10

Steve

This part of my story might be hard for those with a religious mindset—the idea of watching a baseball game in Heaven could be unthinkable. But I'm glad God doesn't conform to the image many people have of Him. Our Father is full of life, love, and, yes, fun!

And I believe Jesus has a sense of humor. Think about the men He chose to be His closest disciples. These were not religious men, pious men, learned men, or even priests or rabbis. They were fishermen—earthy, simple, and often blunt. They definitely had some rough edges. And let's not forget about Matthew, the tax collector. Now, he was someone people loved to hate. In fact, the only people Jesus ever complained about were the religious men, not the sinners.

Aren't you glad God doesn't have a religious mindset? He is the source of all wisdom yet is so full of love that He's prepared a place for us with fun activities we'll really enjoy.

After throwing a ball with my son, Daniel, I walked with him and Marzuka toward a towering building near another field. Ted came over to me in the field.

"Want to go to a baseball game?" my brother asked with a smile.

"Sure!" I blurted. "I didn't know there was baseball in Heaven."

The Baseball Game

To my amazement, we were outside a baseball stadium. It was a three-level structure, off-white in color. On its outside were carvings of baseball scenes: a pitcher pitching a ball, a batter swinging a bat, a fielder diving for a ball. Gazing up, I blinked, realizing that the higher levels of the stadium floated above the ground-level portion. I can't fully express what this looked like—they just floated in place.

To enter the stadium, Ted, Daniel, Marzuka, and I walked up a ramp, on a solid material, dark gray in color. Once inside, I saw that all the seats were white with curved backs and a padded material as cushions. The stadium was crowded, and everyone cheered for their teams.

When we took our seats in the lower level, right behind home plate, most of the ones around us were filled. Marzuka sat a couple of rows behind us, and I'm struck now remembering how polite he was. He didn't say anything during the game. He must have known I liked baseball.

I was so surprised that I was watching a baseball game in Heaven. I also wanted to talk to my brother, whom I hadn't seen in so many years.

An umpire wearing a traditional uniform called balls and strikes. Other umpires stood around the bases as well. Batters didn't wear batting helmets, only caps, no doubt because you can't get hurt in Heaven! The catcher didn't wear a mask, and neither did the home plate umpire. One team's hats had a red cap and white bill; the other team's hats had a white cap and red bill.

I saw the players' faces but didn't recognize any of them. They might have been people who just liked to play baseball, or they might have been former players—I wasn't sure. But nobody seemed to care. They just cheered and enjoyed the game as a game.

The scoreboard was unusual because the numbers seemed to float in the air. Above us were a second and third level of seating, with stairways that led up to each level. However, no poles supported the upper decks. They floated in the air too! This was great, because there was nothing to block anyone's view. Every seat was a good seat. In the background, music played, reminiscent of an organ playing at baseball games. None of the tunes were ones I recognized. I did see some people eating food, but I don't know what it was or where they got it.

I'm familiar with different types of baseball pitches: fast-balls, curveballs, sliders, cutters, and changeups. But here, the pitcher could make the ball follow a winding, corkscrew pattern that made it difficult to hit. With some pitches, the ball would loop, and with others, it would rotate in amazing patterns. Watching these pitches was fascinating! Both team pitchers threw the corkscrew pitch several times.

The same rules of baseball we have here applied in the game: three outs per inning, nine innings in all. There was a lot of cheering but no booing.

These are some of the other unique aspects to baseball in Heaven: The dirt didn't stick to any of the players' pants when they slid into bases. It just fell off. Also, no stains of any kind were left on the players' uniforms. Yes, no one needs to do laundry in Heaven. The well-manicured grass just springs back up after players step on it. And the bases are made of gold. Yes, gold!

Ted, Daniel, and I talked about the pitching and how we could see the ball move. We discussed the skill of the good fielders and good hitters. That's how I found out Ted seemed to know about a lot of the players—who they were, where they came from. I don't know if he knew them personally, but he was familiar with their playing ability as he'd seen them play before.

What an amazing thing. Not only did God allow me to see my brother, but He allowed me to go to a baseball game with him. How great and wonderful is our God! His mercy toward us is new every morning. His love and faithfulness never end. I will always treasure these precious moments with my brother and Daniel, knowing there will be many more in eternity.

At the end of the game, the red team had won. The teams shook hands, hugged, and gave each other high fives—but I don't remember the score!

Here we often watch fireworks after a baseball game. In Heaven, we watched a "light show." There were dazzling colors, shapes, and such artistry in the sky. It was better than any fireworks I've ever seen. God is the creator of light, so why wouldn't His light shows be the best?

After the show, the three of us and Marzuka walked out of the stadium together. Ted said he had some things to do, but he didn't tell me what they were. Daniel said he was going to play with friends. (Daniel had also said Jesus often comes to play with the children. What an amazing Savior! He cares for every child and makes each one feel special.)

Ted and I hugged goodbye and said it was good to see each other. Daniel and I hugged and expressed our love. Then we quietly parted. Different roads, made of white gold, went in separate directions outside the stadium. Ted went down one, Daniel another, and Marzuka and I took a third path.

If you have loved ones in Heaven, you can be assured that they're waiting for you. They're excited about the fantastic things you'll do together as you enjoy what God has prepared for you. Your family members who have passed on are now in your future, and that future is bright and filled with exciting things for you to do. Heaven is so much greater and better than anything we have here on Earth. There are so many heavenly places to explore. We will have eternity to enjoy our favorite pastimes. Just having a small glimpse of the world called Heaven makes me want to glorify God and worship Him for His goodness. No pleasure here can compare with what Heaven has to offer.

As I followed my angelic guide, we walked into a picture-perfect scene. More about that in the next chapter, but first, a little update from Kathy's perspective.

Kathy

While Steve was enjoying a baseball game in Heaven, in the hospital his body was certainly in the shadow of death. As I mentioned earlier, since he was intubated and ventilated, I couldn't communicate with him. During the first twenty days when I wasn't allowed to visit him, I would ask his nurse to FaceTime me with Steve's phone so I could see him, speak Scriptures to him, and pray for him. The first time his nurse set up the FaceTime connection, seeing Steve intubated, sedated, and on the ventilator was shocking. Although I knew what to expect from my training, I still felt devastated as I saw my sweet husband, still and helpless, relying on a machine to breathe for him.

I had to muster all the courage I could to begin reading the Scriptures. But as I did, I grew stronger on the inside. I focused on every word in these verses and said them emphatically. Sometimes I would pause and read a particular verse again just to let the enemy know I was not backing down. Often I would pause after a verse to pray specifically for the promise noted in it. This process took about forty-five to sixty minutes, depending on how many times I repeated certain Scriptures.

During these FaceTime calls, I would talk to Steve as well. I spoke to him just as if we were having a conversation at the dinner table. I would tell him how my day had been, what Stacie was doing, what I ate, if I slept, and who I spoke with that day. I knew the things that might make him smile and laugh, so I was sure to include anything he would find humorous. I wondered what the nurses and therapists who came in and out of Steve's room thought about all this. However, their opinions didn't really matter to me. I was fighting a battle—a battle that belonged to the Lord. I knew I just had to stand in faith and that God was responsible for the outcome.

In our more than thirty years of marriage, Steve has been strong and steady in many ways. When I got nervous, he could always calm me down. In fact, Steve never really worried about anything. He obeyed Philippians 4:6 better than anyone I've known: "Don't worry about anything; instead, pray about everything. Tell God what you need, and thank him for all he has done" (NLT). When we were first married, one day I asked Steve if he really cared about me, or about anything, because he never worried. I found it astonishing that he could be so positive all the time and never even entertain the thought of a negative outcome. I learned over the years that he did care; he just didn't worry.

While on the ventilator, Steve could no longer tell me not to worry. His soothing voice and wonderful sense of humor had been silenced. It was now my faith and trust in God that mattered. I had to walk through this valley and not stop and meditate on the deathly shadows around me.

To counter all the negative thoughts and doubts that tried to flood my mind on a regular basis, I spoke out Bible verses daily. In fact, I created a four-page document with healing Scriptures that I prayed and spoke every day. (Those Scriptures are included for you in the appendix at the back of this book.)

Psalm 23 tells us that God's rod and staff comfort us. How does a shepherd use a rod and staff? He uses the rod to beat off predators. It's a type of weapon. He uses the staff to hook around a sheep stuck in a thicket and pull it out. We know Jesus has already defeated our predator—Satan—but we must stand strong in the victory Jesus has already won.

First Peter 5:8–9 says, "Stay alert! Watch out for your great enemy, the devil. He prowls around like a roaring lion, looking for someone to devour. Stand firm against him and be strong in your faith" (NLT). It doesn't matter what your situation is; Jesus can pull you out. His staff is far-reaching. Keep praying, and don't give up!

My mother's favorite hymn was "Great Is Thy Faithfulness."[1] Even now, those words are so powerful:

> Great is Thy faithfulness, O God, my Father;
> There is no shadow of turning with Thee;
> Thou changest not, Thy compassions, they fail not;
> As Thou hast been, Thou forever wilt be.
> Great is Thy faithfulness!
> Great is Thy faithfulness!
> Morning by morning, new mercies I see;
> All I have needed, Thy hand hath provided:
> Great is Thy faithfulness, Lord, unto me!

The Lord does have compassion on us, His children. Just as we, as parents, love our children and want the best for them, God our Father loves us and wants the best for us. Although we often don't understand why we face so many problems, we know we have a Father who loves us and will turn situations around for our good when we trust Him. This is a key to answered prayer.

---

1. Thomas Chisholm wrote this well-known Christian hymn as a poem in 1923 and sent it to William Runyan, who then set it to music. It was published that same year by Hope Publishing. Billy Graham often used the song during his international crusades, and it entered the public domain in 2019.

Remember, our enemy is always trying to make us doubt God and what God has said. The snake started this tactic in the garden of Eden and has never changed his strategy. He planted doubt in Eve's mind: "Hath God said . . ." (Genesis 3:1 KJV). The devil always includes a morsel of truth in the lies he tells us. It's never the whole truth. In Steve's case, the truth was that he was critically ill in the ICU and might die. However, the truth also was and is that Jesus is the one "who Himself bore our sins in His own body on the tree, that we, having died to sins, might live for righteousness—by whose stripes you were healed" (1 Peter 2:24).

8

A Tour, Warhorses, and Angels Unaware

STEVE AND KATHY

He showed me a pure river of water of life.

Revelation 22:1

The horse is prepared for the day of battle, but deliverance is of the LORD.

Proverbs 21:31

Do not forget to entertain strangers, for by so doing some have unwittingly entertained angels.

Hebrews 13:2

Steve

After I said goodbye to Ted and Daniel, Marzuka told me we were going to a worship center. Then we walked down a wide road made of clear, pure gold. On either side of the road were large buildings with pristine landscaping. After passing three groups of them, we turned to our right on another golden street that led us to a large U-shaped stadium. We walked through one of its tall archways and onto the grassy field it surrounded, joining tens of thousands of people. The stadium held a massive choir and orchestra. Although I was standing far away from them, my vision was clear and my focus precise.

Praise Music

As Marzuka and I stood in the crowd, I noticed Kathy's mom, Eileen, standing near us, to our left. I waved at her and she waved back. The choir filled the left half of the U-shaped stadium. To my amazement, I saw my mother and grandmother in the choir. The thousands of singers all wore white robes. And I saw Kathy's father sitting in the first violin section of the massive orchestra, which filled the right side of the stadium.

As the conductor raised his arms, a hush fell over the crowd, and then the orchestra started playing with perfect intonation. No need for tuning these instruments! The choir joined them in song, and I recognized the melodies of Handel's *Messiah*. As the multitude sang and played, I noticed many angels flying overhead, forming an amazing dome of angelic host. Although I had no sense of time as we worshiped, I never tired of listening to the heavenly music, worshiping God, and standing in the plush green field of this worship center.

The Mountains

After the amazing worship service, Marzuka and I walked along a ten-foot-wide, smooth, dirt-like trail into the mountains, and

I noticed there were no snowcaps on their peaks. I commented about the lush green appearance of these mountains as we walked among a forest of trees, but there was no tree line like you'd see in the Rocky Mountains. These mountains had grass and trees all the way up to the top. The "dirt" on the ground didn't stick to our feet or sandals; it merely fell off with each step we took. I even hesitate to call it dirt as this was not an earthly environment; this was Heaven.

As we discussed the beauty of the green mountain peaks, Marzuka spoke about the importance of our words, just as my dad had mentioned in his carving room.

"In Heaven you can literally create your environment with your words," he said. "If you wanted snowcaps on the mountains, you could speak to the mountains, and snow would appear."

Again, Mark 11:23 flooded my mind. In that verse, Jesus tells us to speak to our mountains here on Earth. He was teaching us heavenly principles and the power of our words, especially when we believe in our heart what we say with our mouth.

With Marzuka still on my left side, we headed toward one of the mountain peaks. As we journeyed up the trail, Marzuka said, "You've been here a while and haven't eaten anything. Are you hungry?"

"Yes, I could eat something. Do you have any suggestions?" I asked. I hadn't yet visited my mother's home and eaten the cake she had for me.

"How about this?" Marzuka replied as he handed me a copper-colored fruit about the size of a grapefruit. The fruit was delicious, and I immediately felt strengthened as I ate it. When I finished it, Marzuka had another surprise for me. He handed me a cone of vanilla ice cream, my favorite flavor. What a treat! It tasted amazing. I can honestly say it was the best vanilla ice cream I've ever had.

Refreshed and strengthened, I followed Marzuka across a dazzling mountain stream on a bridge about ten feet long, with no rails. At the top of the mountain were still plenty of trees and no large rocks or boulders. We stood in a clearing where the view was fantastic. Behind us in the distance was the meadow. Beyond the meadow was the city where I'd met my parents and Kathy's parents. To our left was a forest of trees. To our right was the mountain range with peaks as far as I could see. When we lived in Colorado, I would take our three huskies—Yaz, Brooks, and Pete—for hikes up Barr Trail at Pikes Peak. This mountain hike reminded me of Barr Trail, only much more stunning.

"This view is spectacular," I said in awe and wonder.

"All of God's creation is spectacular," Marzuka responded.

The Valley

Leaving the clearing, we turned to our right and went down a trail leading to a V-shaped valley. It was a meandering path, like switchbacks. Toward the bottom, we got off the mountain path and walked along the floor of the valley—a stunning plateau with trees like pine trees and all kinds of flowers. The flowers had multicolored petals, just like the ones I'd seen in the meadow, and were grouped together in beds. The trees covered a large expanse, like a forest. Marzuka and I walked for about a mile, birds flying and singing overhead. It was bright, but there was no glare and there were no shadows. Then we turned around and retraced our steps to the mountain path.

Marzuka said, "I have another place to take you."

The River

We resumed our downward trek, and in the distance, I could see a river.

Marzuka said, "This is the River of Life."

As I looked out over the water, it seemed to sparkle, and it was amazingly clear. Several people stood in the river, splashing and enjoying the beautiful crystal water. Across the river, I saw another sandy beach lined with palm trees.

As we walked toward the river, I noticed it was wide and on this side had a white sandy beach. I saw many palm tree groves there, each one with three to five trees.

I said, "I love palm trees!"

"I know!" Marzuka replied. "That's why I brought you here. I've been on many beach vacations with you."

The water remained clear with gentle waves as we walked in the sand.

"This is great!" I said. "I didn't know there were beaches like this in Heaven."

"You need to broaden your imagination regarding what's here," Marzuka replied.

Despite the brightness of the sky, the light didn't hurt my eyes or my skin. There was no need for sunglasses or sunscreen. I stood under a grove of palm trees, enjoying the gentle breeze and taking in the gorgeous scene. This was better than any beach I'd been to, and I wanted to hang out here for a while.

As we left the beach, I realized that Marzuka had taken me to the four places pictured in the carvings on the wall of the Welcome Center: the meadow, the mountains, the valley, and the groves of palm trees.

We took a path off the beach toward a hill. This path was ten feet wide and made of a solid silvery material I somehow knew was white gold. On either side of the course was a grassy area with broad trees, sixty to seventy feet tall, scattered throughout the region. Birds sang from the treetops, a grand chorus of creation.

Then I followed Marzuka off the path onto a dirt-like surface and walked up a gently rolling hill. All around us, grass and trees filled the landscape, with wildflowers of red, blue, yellow, purple, and green dotting the green landscape. Once we reached the crest of the hill, a massive complex of monumental buildings came into view, all white and made of a material unknown to me.

The Warhorses of Heaven

As we drew closer, heading down the opposite side of the hill, the buildings became more distinct, like a photo coming into focus. Stables with intricate carvings of horses on the walls towered above the magnificent scenery. These carvings—relief carvings—were made of smoky white pearl material. One of the scenes had several horses running together; another had an adult horse and a pony together. Some carvings showed horses running and others standing.

Pausing to get my bearings, I scanned the area and was taken aback by the immensity of the grassy field surrounding the stables and the grandeur of the building in front of them.

The sound of gentle but firm thuds came just over the horizon from an area where horses were practicing maneuvers. Then the area near the stables was peaceful as the horses reached the large door to the stables. Though it appeared to be wood, it seemed more solid than wood. It opened automatically like a double sliding door, and a couple of angels passed in and out of the doorway.

Marzuka and I entered, and horse stalls filled the space as far as I could see. Then, turning right, we passed multiple aisles with stalls made of a dark, smooth, wood-type material on either side. They were about forty feet by forty feet, large enough for each incredible horse. The stall doors were like Dutch doors, the bottom closed and the top open. Each door's top part was made of vertical silver-colored bars about four to five inches apart. The floor the horses strode upon was dirt, but the dirt didn't stick to them. Each stall door had a horse's name, but the names didn't register as we advanced on.

As stunning as the architecture was, excitement shot through me when I saw some horses pawing at the ground and snorting restlessly, others being brushed by angels, and some eating out of troughs in their stalls. Although I have limited knowledge of horses, I'm familiar with a few distinct types, especially Clydesdales—large draught horses that can be well over two thousand pounds and very muscular, able to pull heavy loads.

I've also seen thoroughbreds, though not as large and usually bred for speed. However, these horses were both muscular and fast. They blew and snorted with excitement. Each was five to five-and-a-half feet tall at the withers (shoulders), and every one of them was pure white and beautiful. When they moved, their muscles flexed. Their deep blue eyes were calm and still. Their tails were full and flowing. Their hooves were white.

Their majesty and power were breathtaking, and they looked determined and ready for action. Cautiously, I approached one of the stalls, admiring the grandeur and splendor of the heavenly creature. The strong desire to touch the animal was quenched by the knowledge that it was not the

97

right or appropriate thing to do. Marzuka motioned to me, and we kept walking.

Now we passed angels in white robes with gold trim grooming horses. Though these angels didn't have wings, it was apparent they were important ones working to prepare the horses for something.

We stopped at one particular horse, and the angel brushing it smiled at me, then spoke to the horse in a gentle, soothing voice. Marzuka and that angel launched into a dialogue in a language I couldn't understand. By the tone of their voices, though, it sounded like a casual exchange; they seemed to know each other. During the conversation, the brushing angel looked at me and nodded.

Moving on, we walked through the building and saw another cluster of horses fitted with armor. The armor was made of a mesh type, a brilliant silver, and seemed lightweight yet incredibly strong and protective. It covered their chests, flank areas, and necks.

I wanted to stop and take it all in, but Marzuka kept moving, urging me outside into the large field behind the stables. It was the size of fifteen to twenty football fields, flat and full of lush green grass that sprang back up when the horses stepped on it. Moving into the field, I couldn't count the number of horses training in formation, doing what could only be described as military maneuvers. Angels rode these saddled white horses, wearing white robes that seemed to surround each leg as wide pants would. They all had gold sashes and gold trim on the robes. Some angels had swords in sheaths across their backs; others had bows and arrows, also carried across their backs. I noted that while the horses wore armor, the angels did not. I suddenly stopped walking when it hit me: They were preparing for a future battle.

Standing in awe and amazement at the facility's enormity, the animals' beauty, the great care being given, and the measured, respectful training from the angels, I was frozen, my mind spinning with questions.

Marzuka seemed to have read my thoughts. He told me, "These are the Lord's warhorses. He created them for one purpose: to fight the enemy. They can't be hurt, and they won't die. The armor is more for show."

That brought Revelation 19:11–14 to mind:

> Now I saw heaven opened, and behold, a white horse. And He who sat on him was called Faithful and True, and in righteousness He judges and makes war. He was clothed with a robe dipped in blood, and His name is called The Word of God. And the armies in heaven, clothed in fine linen, white and clean, followed Him on white horses.

"What will happen to these horses after the battle?" I asked.

"The Lord will give them as a reward to those who love Him," he responded.

After we saw the warhorses practicing their maneuvers, Marzuka said, "Let's go back to the stables. We're going to do something you'll enjoy."

As we walked into one of the stable buildings, Marzuka led us to the stall where we'd previously encountered his angelic friend. Marzuka and the other angel spoke briefly, again in a language I couldn't understand. Then we walked over to two majestic steeds wearing white saddles, ready to ride. My saddle had a red cross on each side. Suddenly, I found myself on the horse, and Marzuka was on the other horse. He led us outside, and we rode side by side on a winding path that encircled the entire complex.

Sometimes the horses trotted, but other times they broke into a full gallop. For these horses, even a gallop seemed effortless. I rode comfortably even though I'm not used to riding horses. These horses knew exactly what to do. We rode through beautiful countryside, picture-perfect scenes of trees, flowers, and grass. Again, I was overwhelmed by the brilliance of color in God's creation. The bright blue sky was completely cloudless.

Upon returning to the stables, I found myself standing next to my horse and gently stroking this amazing creature. There was no hint of fatigue, either in the horses or me.

More About Marzuka

When we left the stables, Marzuka and I walked down another golden street. I asked him how long he'd been with the Lord, and he said he'd been there from the beginning and serves at the Lord's command. He'd been assigned to me as a guardian and saved my life on many occasions, even when I wasn't aware of a clear danger. This time the Lord had sent him to bring my spirit to Heaven while my body healed on Earth.

"Sometimes I take human form to perform an assignment," he noted. "Everyone has a guardian, but the guardian is limited in what can be done for a person if he or she hasn't accepted the Lord as Savior."

"Do you ever use your sword?" I asked.

"The sword is for spiritual battles," he replied.

"What does it look like?"

Marzuka took the sheath off his back, held it in his left hand, and grabbed the handle of the sword with his right hand. He pulled the sword out about six to seven inches. In the middle of the blade was an artistic swirling design, and the edges of the sword had a golden glow. Marzuka explained that these edges could cut through anything. I asked him why the sheath isn't cut by the sword. He told me it has a special lining that protects it. Then just as deftly as he'd removed the sword, he replaced it, and we resumed our walk.

"I want to take you to a very special place," he said, and our pace picked up.

Now back for a moment to Kathy, who had an angelic encounter of her own.

Kathy

During my Pediatric residency in St. Louis, I had a supernatural experience with an angel. My program allowed us to take five glorious days off either around Christmas or New Year's, a welcome break from our usual eighty- to one-hundred-hour per week work schedule. The night before my holiday vacation, I worked until about 10:30 p.m., then drove home to my apartment complex. We'd had a significant snowstorm, and I found the nearby parking lot completely full, the only available space covered with an elevated pile of snow. Incredibly tired and thinking only of catching my plane to Tulsa in the morning, I pulled my little Subaru up onto the snowbank.

What a foolish idea! Now my car was suspended on a snow pile. The wheels weren't even touching the ground. All I could do was spin them when I pressed on the accelerator. I was in trouble! How would I get to the airport in the morning? Even if I took a cab to and from the airport, how could I get to work when I returned to St. Louis if the snow pile was still there?

I called my automobile association and was told they couldn't pull my car out as it wasn't on a city street. I called my parents in Tulsa, crying. Daddy kept telling me to put something under the tires to get traction. Frustrated, I explained that the tires wouldn't touch the ground no matter what I put under them.

I called Steve as well, but he didn't have any other ideas.

Chronic fatigue had taken its toll both on my physical body and my emotions as I stood there in the cold, but I repented for my foolishness and, in desperation, cried out to the Lord and asked Him to help me.

"Ya need some help?"

Suddenly, I saw headlights coming toward me and experienced a peaceful feeling as a white pickup stopped right in front of me.

A very tall man got out, looked directly at me, and said, "Ya need some help?"

"Yes!" I replied. "I did a stupid thing and drove my car up onto the snow. Now it's stuck."

"That's no problem," he said. "I can pull it right out."

To my amazement, this man hooked my car up to his truck and pulled it right off that embankment.

Remember, I was super tired from my grueling schedule, so in the moment I didn't really think this through. But how did he know I needed help? I didn't recognize him even though he seemed to know me. And as far as I can remember, he wore a flannel-type shirt and said, "Ya need some help?" in a distinctively Southern accent.

I can't explain how I know he knew me, but he did. Really, who else would unexpectedly be driving into a parking lot to help me at 11 p.m. at night? He knew where I lived and that I needed help.

After he pulled my car off the snow, I thanked him profusely. As a poor resident, I didn't have any money to give him, but I wanted to do something to show my gratitude. I asked him where he lived. In reply, he pointed directly at my apartment.

Confused, I said, "You can't live there. That's where I live. You must live somewhere else. Well, anyway, if you ever want a cup of coffee or something, please come over . . ."

I was rambling, and it never occurred to me to ask him what his name was. Quietly, he waved, told me goodbye, got back in his white truck, and drove off. My thoughts drifted back to finding a parking space for my car. This time I parked far away from my apartment in a space that had no snow.

Only sometime later did I realize my encounter that night had to be with an angel. I believe it was my guardian angel. I had just asked God to help me when the headlights showed up, coming toward me at exactly the right time. The more I thought about what happened, the more I realized again the depth of God's love for me. Despite my foolishness, the Lord saved me and kept me safe.

I never felt fear or concern that this stranger might have bad intentions. There was only peace in my heart when I met him.

Angels Unaware

Sometimes angels come in the form of strangers. Hebrews 13:2 tells us, "Don't forget to show hospitality to strangers, for some who have done this have entertained angels without realizing it!" (NLT). And Isaiah 65:24 says, "I will answer them before they even call to me. While they are still talking about their needs, I will go ahead and answer their prayers!" (NLT). I had just called out to the Lord when that angel came driving into the parking lot to pull my car out of the snow.

What an amazing God we have! He genuinely cares about everything that concerns us. And He will answer our prayers even before we say the "Amen." Start believing and trusting God, and He will do the same for you.

9

The Throne Room

STEVE

Immediately I was in the Spirit; and behold, a throne set in heaven, and One sat on the throne. And He who sat there was like a jasper and a sardius stone in appearance; and there was a rainbow around the throne, in appearance like an emerald.

Revelation 4:2–3

Marzuka and I walked down another street in Heaven, different from the street where we saw my parents and Kathy's. On our left was a beautiful river, and I instinctively knew this was still the river of water of life, which, as I said in the Introduction to this book, is often called the River of Life. It was narrower here than the part of Heaven I'd seen when we left the valley, but it was lined with beautiful palm trees, tall and majestic, and more people swam and played in the water. Joy and laughter emanated from them.

Soon the river passed out of sight, and I could see a tall building at the end of the street. It was made of white pearl and full of carvings of animals and palm trees. Embedded in the pearl walls were beautiful gemstones, and an arched door made of white gold opened as we approached.

Marzuka and I walked into a large hallway with twenty-foot-high ceilings that stretched about fifty feet in length. The walls were embedded with precious stones. At the end of the hallway was the Throne Room.

I immediately felt excitement coursing through me. Recalling all this, I realize I felt no sense of fear or unworthiness; I knew I was supposed to be there. I was simply in awe of this place and felt safe, welcomed, protected, and loved.

As I entered the Throne Room, I saw the floor was crystal clear and the walls had precious stones embedded in them. And thunder and lightning filled the room, but it wasn't like a storm here. There was so much power and glory in that place! Behind God's throne was a curved wall from which the lightning issued. Job 26:14 says, "But the thunder of his power who can understand?" (KJV). And Psalm 77:18 states, "The voice of thy thunder was in the heaven: the lightnings lightened the world: the earth trembled and shook" (KJV).

In the book of Revelation, John tells us about his encounters with thunder:

Out of the Throne proceeded lightnings and thunderings and voices. (Revelation 4:5 KJV)

The Lamb opened one of the seals, and I heard, as it were the noise of thunder, one of the four beasts saying, Come and see. (Revelation 6:1 KJV)

I heard a voice from heaven, as the voice of many waters, and as the voice of a great thunder. (Revelation 14:2 KJV)

And in Job 37:2–5 we read:

Hear attentively the thunder of His voice, and the rumbling that comes from His mouth. He sends it forth under the whole heaven, His lightning to the ends of the earth. After it a voice roars; He thunders with His majestic voice. And He does not restrain them when His voice is heard. God thunders marvelously with His voice.

Despite the thunder and lightning in God's presence, I felt completely at peace and totally loved. For "God is love" (1 John 4:16), and "there is no fear in love; but perfect love casts out fear" (verse 18).

Then I saw seven steps that led up to the throne in the middle of the room, where God the Father sat. His appearance was pure light, and I couldn't make out His features as the light was so bright. In Revelation 4:3, John tells us what he saw in his vision of Heaven: "He who sat there [God] was like a jasper and a sardius stone in appearance."

Seated at the Father's right hand was Jesus, our Savior.

This was truly the climax of my journey to Heaven. Seeing the Father and His Son—no words can really describe it. But now I understand what Paul meant when he said, "Since you have been raised to new life with Christ, set your sights on the realities of heaven, where Christ sits in the place of honor at God's right hand" (Colossians 3:1 NLT).

Before I tell you what else I saw in the Throne Room, let me share what God and Christ did for me there. How could I ever forget it?

God and Jesus Spoke to Me

As I listened to the thunder, I heard the voice of God.

"Hello, Steve. Welcome to Heaven."

What I initially heard as thunder had now become a voice—the voice of God. It was deep and strong. I was speechless. It was a "thunder-voice," as Psalm 18:13 describes: "The great God above every god spoke with His thunder-voice from the sky. The Most High uttered his voice!" (TPT). The Father's voice sounds like thunder!

Look at John 12:28–29, where Jesus said, "Father, bring glory to Your name," before the passage goes on: "Then a voice spoke from heaven, saying, 'I have already brought glory to my name, and I will do so again.' When the crowd heard the voice, some thought it was thunder, while others declared an angel had spoken to him" (NLT).

In that moment, I could feel the reality of being covered by the blood of Jesus and having my sins washed away, and I knew the Father had called me up to Heaven. I had a tremendous sense of anticipation as I stood before Him.

What happened next was truly overwhelming. Jesus stood and walked down the steps to me. Then as He looked at me with eyes full of love, He said, "I want to show you something."

Jesus pointed to His right, and through a portal I saw my physical body lying face down with my head turned to the right. My skin was gray, and I wore gray striped pajamas. I didn't see any details of the room I was in. There was no hospital bed, no machines, and no IV poles—just the gray-colored body.

"This is you, but you're going to be all right," Jesus told me. Then after a brief pause, He said, "I have something else to show you."

Once again, I looked to Jesus' right and saw my body, but this time, though it remained in the same position, I now had color in my skin. I looked normal, and I wore different pajamas. Instead of gray stripes, these pajamas had red and white stripes.

"You're going to be just fine. The red is My blood, and the white is My righteousness," Jesus said. "You're healed by My blood and My righteousness."

I was overcome with emotion, but said, "Praise you, Lord, for your goodness and your blood and your sacrifice."

Jesus reached toward me and gave me a hug. I cannot adequately explain what it feels like to be hugged by the Son of God. But if you know Jesus, you'll find out someday for yourself. There was so much love in that embrace—it was tangible!

Then Jesus put His hands on my shoulders and looked into my eyes. His eyes looked blue and were deep and beautiful. His complexion was dark olive. He had a well-trimmed beard and flowing shoulder-length dark brown hair. He wore a white robe with a purple sash. In my peripheral vision, I noticed the scars at the base of His hands. His demeanor was calm, and His love was palpable.

He said, "I love you. I have work for you to do after you return, and I'll let you know what it is at the right time."

Acknowledging His powerful words, I simply replied, "Okay." Being a bit overwhelmed, I was at a loss for words.

"You saw My stables and My warhorses preparing for battle," Jesus stated.

"When will this happen, Lord?" I asked.

"Very soon."

The Lord showed me one more thing before I left. In my younger days, I played the drums and really enjoyed it. Six years prior to being in Heaven, I experienced disappointment regarding an opportunity to play drums for worship. At that time, the Lord told me one day I would be playing drums for Him. Now, as I stood beside my King, He showed me a large drum set with many drums made of white pearl and cymbals of gold.

"These drums are for you to play when you get here," Jesus said.

What a wonderful Lord we serve! He cares about everything that concerns us. He sees everything and knows us intimately, He never lets our disappointments go unnoticed, and He'll fulfill our heart's desire when we serve Him.

Just as Scripture Tells Us

Here's what else I saw in the Throne Room:

The elders

In Revelation 4:4, John mentions "twenty-four thrones" and says, "On the thrones I saw twenty-four elders." When I entered the Throne Room, on either side of the thrones of God and Jesus, I, too, saw twelve elders sitting on thrones—each dressed in a white robe—for a total of twenty-four elders.

The ark of the covenant and the menorah

I saw the ark of the covenant and the menorah to the Father's left. Hebrews 9:24 tells us, "Christ did not enter into a holy place made with human hands, which was only a copy of the true one in heaven. He entered into heaven itself to appear now before God on our behalf" (NLT). This was the real ark of the covenant, the original one. Israel's ark of the covenant was a copy of the eternal ark. Hebrews 9:12 tells us, "Not with the blood of goats and calves, but with His own blood He entered the Most Holy Place once for all, having obtained eternal redemption."

A *rainbow*

Above God's throne was a rainbow—God's symbol of covenant He gave Noah:

> And God said . . . "I set My rainbow in the cloud, and it shall be for the sign of the covenant between Me and the earth. It shall be, when I bring a cloud over the earth, that the rainbow shall be seen in the cloud; and I will remember My covenant which is between Me and you and every living creature of all flesh; the waters shall never again become a flood to destroy all flesh. The rainbow shall be in the cloud and I will look on it to remember the everlasting covenant between God and every living creature of all flesh that is on the earth." And God said to Noah, "This is the sign of the covenant which I have established between Me and all flesh that is on the earth."
>
> Genesis 9:12–17

I Return to Earth

After Jesus spoke to me, in a flash, Marzuka and I were walking out the door.

"I need to get you back because you'll be waking up soon," he said. "And Kathy will be waiting for you."

Together we walked back to the Welcome Center, and the same man was behind the desk.

"Bye, Steve," he said.

Then Marzuka looked at me, smiled, and nodded as he said, "I'll be around if you need me."

Suddenly, I was traveling through space at great speed, headed for Earth. Before a thought could pass through my mind, I was back in my body, in the hospital bed, and I opened my eyes for the first time in several weeks.

There was my sweet wife, Kathy, waiting for me, just as Marzuka said. Except for the first twenty days of my hospitalization, she'd been physically at my side every day and as much as she could.

It would be weeks before I remembered my journey to Heaven. Little did I know the incredible challenges and difficult path to recovery that lay ahead. But in the days that followed, I would find comfort in the words of the apostle Paul: "And He said to me, 'My grace is sufficient for you, for My strength is made perfect in weakness.' Therefore most gladly I will rather boast in my infirmities, that the power of Christ may rest upon me" (2 Corinthians 12:9).

10

Answered Prayers

KATHY

Therefore I say to you, whatever things you ask when you pray, believe that you receive them, and you will have them.

Mark 11:24

Answered prayers are powerful. The moment Steve's eyes opened—while he was still intubated and on the ventilator—my heart filled with gratitude to God for bringing him back to me. He'd been in a coma for three weeks.

I so clearly remember the moment he saw me. His eyes got really big and expressive, and I knew he wanted to tell me something. He couldn't, but he was obviously happy to see me, and I was so glad he was awake.

Little did I know where he'd been for so many weeks, Earth time.

From this point on, Steve would be awake for a good part of the day, but he couldn't speak while intubated, or even later with the tracheostomy, since he was still connected to the ventilator. This was incredibly frustrating for him, so we tried multiple ways of communication:

Letters on a page he could point to and spell out words. But most of the time his hands were too weak to do this.

His mouthing words slowly so I could try to read his lips. But that didn't work very well.

And a game of "multiple guessing," when I would name off a list of things I thought he might be trying to tell me, hoping I'd hit one.

Steve was continually frustrated as most of the time we didn't know what he was trying to tell us.

Tubes and More Tubes

By January 4, Steve had been intubated for twenty-one days. That's about the limit for having an endotracheal tube sitting on the vocal cords. Although aware of the possible damage this tube can do, I hoped Steve could be weaned from the ventilator before he needed a more permanent tube with a tracheostomy. Since the tracheostomy tube is placed through the skin in the neck directly into the trachea, there is no damage to the vocal cords. However, that's usually a long-term intervention, and I couldn't imagine Steve having a tracheostomy for weeks or months.

But Steve was fighting Acinetobacter pneumonia and couldn't wean from the ventilator, so I consented to the tracheostomy on January 6. Since the orogastric feeding tube was attached to the endotracheal tube, which was being removed, Steve needed another feeding tube—nasogastric—placed through his nose that went down his esophagus into his stomach.

I waited in the hospital's Family Room while the pulmonologist performed the tracheostomy procedure. With a few round tables, a refrigerator, a counter with a microwave, and cabinets, it was empty of people but for me. I stood staring out the wall of windows, crying out to God in prayer while the afternoon sun warmed me.

From those windows I could see part of the DoubleTree hotel. This was where we spent our wedding night. It was also where we had a romantic weekend two years ago. I remembered our walk on the path behind the hotel, where we shared our hopes and dreams for the future and affirmed our love for each other. Now I prayed from the depths of my heart that God would allow Steve and me to spend another weekend at that hotel and enjoy the love He'd given us.

God was hearing my prayers. As Steve recovered from the Acinetobacter pneumonia, he started breathing trials—times off the regular ventilator settings with the machine in assist mode. This meant Steve would have to initiate his breath and the ventilator would assist in pushing it into his lungs. The safety was that the ventilator would give him a minimum number of breaths per minute even if he didn't initiate them. To come off the ventilator, Steve would need to breathe on his own with good oxygen saturation and keep his heart rate and blood pressure stable.

Every day was a roller coaster. Steve would do well for a while and then suddenly need more ventilatory support. His labs would trend toward normal one day, and the next day his white blood cell count and inflammatory markers would soar. It was unending ups and downs. His vital signs would be normal during the day and then be unstable all night. As soon as one thing improved, something else went wrong.

The only stabilizing force was Jesus. I learned a great deal about faith during this time, as did Steve. (We'll share these insights in a chapter still ahead.)

Just as the endotracheal tube couldn't stay for the long haul, the nasogastric tube needed to come out, also to prevent complications. On January 12 I consented to a gastrostomy tube placement for long-term feedings that went directly into Steve's stomach through the abdominal wall. Each time I consented to a new procedure, I had to remind myself that God would make a way for these devices to be removed, and that Steve would be perfectly normal at some point in the future, no matter what he looked like at that moment.

Facing Our Goliaths

As you can see, once Steve's eyes were open, our journey back to his total health had only just begun. From that moment on, however, we were in the fight together. Up to this point, it had been me against my Goliath, strengthened by the Word of God in my heart and in my mouth.

The story of David and Goliath in 1 Samuel 17 has taken on new meaning for me. In this powerful story, we see the fantastic audacity of this young man as he spoke out his beliefs in the face of his nation's number one enemy: a giant named Goliath.

> David said to the Philistine, "You come to me with a sword, with a spear, and with a javelin. But I come to you in the name of the LORD of hosts, the God of the armies of Israel, whom you have defied. This day the LORD will deliver you into my hand, and I

will strike you and take your head from you. And this day I will give the carcasses of the camp of the Philistines to the birds of the air and the wild beasts of the earth, that all the earth may know that there is a God in Israel. Then all this assembly shall know that the LORD does not save with sword and spear; for the battle *is* the LORD's, and He will give you into our hands."

1 Samuel 17:45–47

One of the major giants we face today is sickness. With Steve in the ICU, I had to fight this Goliath both in the hospital room and in my prayer room. I was one of millions fighting this way. But I'm emboldened by the fact that we pray to, serve, and love a God who has extensive experience with rescuing people from impossible situations through the power of His Word. The Bible is full of such accounts. Often, He uses the most unlikely people, like David.

David was the youngest in his family. And when the prophet Samuel came to his father, Jesse, to anoint the future king of Israel, Jesse presented only the seven oldest of his eight sons. He hoped one of them would be chosen.

When Samuel looked at Jesse's first son, Eliab, he thought he must be the anointed one because of his striking physical appearance. Yet Eliab wasn't God's choice: "The Lord said to Samuel, 'Do not look at his appearance or at his physical stature, because I have refused him. For the LORD does not see as man sees; for man looks at the outward appearance, but the LORD looks at the heart'" (1 Samuel 16:7).

After the other six sons had paraded before Samuel, the prophet asked Jesse if he had any more sons. Jesse answered, "There remains yet the youngest, and there he is, keeping the sheep" (verse 11). Now, David was a lowly shepherd—not a profession held in high regard then. Yet this scorned, ill-regarded young man was who God chose to become king of Israel.

Remember David if you wonder what it takes to do great things for the kingdom of God. He came from a low station in life to become a king.

God can use anyone willing to yield to Him. The battles we face daily belong to the Lord. He has already prepared the way for us to overcome every difficult circumstance. It's not our strengths or qualifications that matter. It's what Jesus has already done for us.

We must be willing to stand firm against our enemy, the devil. Many people give up when faced with the giants that challenge us in life. I encourage you to remain steady and trust God and His Word. Remember, God is looking at your heart. He will come through in big things—such as bringing Steve out of the coma—and in small things, such as college exams that stand in the way of your future.

Help from the Holy Spirit

In medical school, I had two exams on the heels of my fiancé breaking off our engagement and realizing I'd disobeyed God's will for my life because I hadn't ended our relationship sooner. As I told you earlier, I was in no state of mind to study. I managed to postpone one exam as my professor had mercy on me, but I had to sit for the other one. It was a pharmacology exam.

Pharmacology is the study of all the prescription drugs we use in medicine. If you've ever looked at the package insert for a prescription medication, you'll notice sections about the drug's chemical structure and mechanisms of action. This is part of pharmacology and is a complex subject. As I tried to study for this exam, I fought to focus. Still, the pain of the breakup made it difficult, and I merely turned the pages in my pharmacology notebook, unable to concentrate.

By this point, I'd become a professional student and learned to calculate what grade I needed on an exam to keep an A in the class. In pharmacology, I figured I needed a 60 percent on this exam to keep a B in the class. As I entered the exam room that day, I prayed for a 60 percent score.

Then the test started. Reading the fifty multiple-choice questions, I realized I couldn't answer any of them. But I tried. By the time I was finished, I had gone through every question and changed my answers about three times.

My reaction was panic, but I calmed myself and remembered it was God who called me to medicine. He would have to provide for me.

I bowed my head in prayer.

Lord, I know I don't deserve this, but right now I ask for your grace and mercy. I ask you, Holy Spirit, to help me. Show me the answers to this exam. In Jesus' name, amen.

I returned to the first question, read it, prayed in the Spirit, and then chose what I thought was the best answer. I repeated this process for all fifty multiple-choice questions. Then I turned in my test.

Test scores were posted on a bulletin board called The Wailing Wall—appropriately named—and listed by Social Security number. (This was before anyone had concerns about stolen identities.) A few days later I rode up the elevator to The Wailing

Wall and prayed even though I thought it was futile as nothing could change my score at this point.

I was astonished when I looked at the posting. My grade was 86 percent. I was speechless! I'd prayed for a 60 percent and got an 86 percent.

While I was still in shock and staring at the board, a classmate came beside me to look at his score. We were chaplains for our class, and he knew about my broken engagement. He asked me what grade I received.

"It's 86 percent."

"Wow, Kathy! That's great! You did a lot better than I did. You must have studied a lot for this exam."

"You have no idea!" I said.

"I know. I studied so many hours for this exam. It was so hard. You did so well!"

"But you have no idea!" I repeated. Struggling to get my thoughts together, I couldn't say more.

"You'll have to tell me how you studied for it."

"Please," I said, interrupting him, "listen to me! I couldn't study for this exam as I was crying so much. I barely turned the pages in my notebook. Then I prayed in the Spirit over each question and asked the Holy Spirit to help me. He helped me find every answer."

"Kathy," he exclaimed, "God really wants you to become a doctor!"

"Yes," I told him. "I know!"

Often, our medical exams included a few controversial questions, and the professor would accept answers that could also be correct. Well, a few of those questions were on this pharmacology exam, so my final grade was an A. I was stunned! I was also humbled and grateful to God for giving me such grace and mercy.

When I speak to student groups and give my testimony, however, I'm always careful to explain that my experience with the grace and mercy of God during that exam does not grant a "free pass" to stop studying. God expects us to be diligent in our studies. Nonetheless, His grace and mercy are always available to us in difficult situations.

Forgiveness Is Available

You may have made mistakes you think are unforgivable. You may have directly disobeyed the Lord, as I did. Maybe you fell into sin through anger. I've done the same. I want you to know that our Father's love for us is more significant than any mistake you've ever made. Jesus stands before you with open arms, waiting for you to receive His love and forgiveness. On His hands are the scars that remind you of the price He paid so you would never have to suffer the consequences of your sins. If you repent and accept His love and forgiveness with a sincere heart, He will forgive all and never remember your mistakes. They are washed away by the blood of Jesus.

This not only happens when you first accept Jesus as your Savior; His forgiveness is there for you every time you sin, even after you've been born again and filled with His Spirit.

The apostle John tells us, "If we say that we have no sin, we deceive ourselves, and the truth is not in us. If we confess our sins, He is faithful and just to forgive us our sins and to cleanse us from all unrighteousness" (1 John 1:8–9). One day I asked the Lord a question about this Scripture in my prayer time. It seemed redundant that He would "forgive us our sins" and "cleanse us from all unrighteousness." Weren't those two actions the same?

The Holy Spirit revealed to me that they're not the same. The first is forgiveness of sins we've committed. The second is cleansing our innate weaknesses for certain types of sin. Each of us is susceptible to certain kinds of sin. What tempts one person is not a temptation for another. Our enemy, Satan, tries to find our weaknesses and tempt us in those areas. For example, if you have a tendency toward addictive behavior, the Lord can cleanse you from that weakness. God can cleanse and remove a weakness that allows us to fall into a particular temptation. In fact, Jesus taught us to pray, "Don't let us yield to temptation, but rescue us from the evil one" (Matthew 6:13 NLT).

The Power of the Holy Spirit, Prayer, Scripture, and Our Words

If we go through a particularly difficult situation and need God's supernatural help, He's there to provide for us each time. His provision is through the Holy Spirit, whom He sent on the day of Pentecost. Jesus said to His disciples, "It is to your advantage that I go away; for if I do not go away, the Helper will not come to you; but if I depart, I will send Him to you" (John 16:7).

Imagine Jesus telling His disciples that it was better for Him to leave and send them the Holy Spirit than for Him to stay with them. In other words, it's better for us to have the Holy Spirit in our lives, helping us in everything God calls us to do, than to have Jesus with us here in the flesh. That's how important the Holy Spirit is!

In this same chapter of John, Jesus says, "However, when He, the Spirit of truth, has come, He will guide you into all truth; for He will not speak on His own authority, but whatever He hears He will speak; and He will tell you things to come" (verse 13). We often don't realize what a gift we have in the Holy Spirit and how important it is for us to know Him. Evangelist Kathryn Kuhlman would say the Holy Spirit was her best friend. He's that still, small voice on the inside that lets you know when something is right—or wrong.

Our Father has many ways to protect and defend His children. Marzuka told Steve that, as his guardian, he had saved his life many times. And sometimes you can't pinpoint why you have a "bad feeling" about a particular situation, but the Lord impresses you to avoid something that could be dangerous. If we listen, the Holy Spirit will tell us things to come. He will tell us what decisions to make and when to say yes or no to every opportunity. God can keep us safe from danger through the leading of His Holy Spirit inside us.

After my experience with the Holy Spirit during my pharmacology exam, I determined to press in and study as hard as possible. I would do my part, and God was responsible for the results. Once again, He was incredibly faithful! The Lord helped me through that pharmacology exam and all my finals and National Board exams with passing grades on everything. This was a significant feat considering what I'd been through emotionally. Some bright medical students in my class failed the Board exams and had to retake them.

But God heard my prayers, and the words that came out of my heart turned the course of my studies and career. I have continued this practice of speaking and praying the Word of God. I believe in its power and witnessed its impact on Steve's health.

As Steve improved in late January, I met one of the nurses who had set up a FaceTime call for me. Steve had not been doing well the last time this nurse saw him. He'd been in a prone position for oxygenation sixteen hours each day with only slight improvement. Now, weeks later, Steve was awake, alert, and recovering from his last and final pneumonia. This nurse remembered all those Scriptures I read to him over FaceTime.

"Wow!" this nurse exclaimed. "I guess all that Scripture reading really helped. It was worth it!"

"Yes, it certainly was!" I responded.

Prayer and Scripture are so powerful. And our words affect the course of our lives. The Bible tells us our tongue is like the rudder of a ship. Although small, it can turn a large vessel:

Horses have bits and bridles in their mouths so that we can control and guide their large body. And the same with mighty ships, though they are massive and driven by fierce winds, yet they are steered by a tiny rudder at the direction of the person at the helm. And so the tongue is a small part of the body yet it carries great power!

James 3:3–5 TPT

11

Road to Recovery

STEVE AND KATHY

Let us run with endurance the race that is set before us, looking unto Jesus, the author and finisher of our faith, who for the joy that was set before Him endured the cross, despising the shame, and has sat down at the right hand of the throne of God.

Hebrews 12:1–2

Steve

When I opened my eyes in early January, still on the ventilator, and saw my precious wife, I was excited. My excitement was short-lived, however; I grew frustrated as I tried to talk and no sound came out. The inability to speak because of the endotracheal tube, and later the tracheostomy, was disheartening.

I've always been an optimist, as well as a patient person, but this recovery tested even my most optimistic attitude. Lying in a hospital bed for months takes its toll on the physical body, not to mention the mental anguish that sets in when one feels helpless for such a long time. Yet 2 Corinthians 9:8 says, "God is able to make all grace abound toward you, that you, always having all sufficiency in all things, may have an abundance for every good work."

I believe God's grace abounded to me in the form of patience and long-suffering. Now I know the Lord has "good work" for me to do for His kingdom on this earth; Jesus told me so. I also learned never to take even the smallest blessing for granted.

From my perspective, let me next tell you about the setbacks yet miracles of my recovery while still in the hospital and on that ventilator. Then Kathy will tell you what she went through as both a wife and doctor. As she already shared, once I was awake again, we were in this fight together. And though our experiences weren't the same, neither of us were ever without Him.

Realizing My Limitations

As I became more aware of my situation, I tried to move various parts of my body. I could wiggle my toes, bend my knees slightly, and move my left hand. But for some reason I couldn't move my right hand no matter how hard I tried. This was quite startling as I'm right-handed and, as a software engineer, use a keyboard daily. Moreover, I couldn't even ask someone why my right hand wouldn't work, since I couldn't talk.

I wondered what could have happened.

A little while later, I pointed to my right hand when the doctor came in. He told me I had "wrist drop" and that it would take some time to get better. Then as he explained that my muscles had atrophied from being in bed for so long, he moved the sheets, and I saw my legs. I was shocked at their appearance! They looked like sticks with skin stretched over them. I was mortified. However, I remembered when I had surgery on my right knee as a teenager. I spent eight weeks with a cast on my right leg, and when the cast was removed, my leg looked like what I was seeing now. Optimistically, I thought, *I got better and stronger then, and I'll get better now.*

Initially, I didn't realize the limitations I had because of all the tubes and machines to which I was connected. I saw the bathroom a few steps away and wondered why I couldn't walk a few steps to use it. And there were so many noises I couldn't escape: the constant piston-like roar of the ventilator; the intermittent, annoying beeping of the IV pumps; and the sound of the alarms on the monitor overhead. But eventually I got used to them. Also, I didn't understand why I wasn't eating anything and wondered why I wasn't hungry.

One thing I really had trouble coping with was a lack of sleep. It wasn't easy to sleep in the daytime with all the doctors, nurses, and therapists coming in and out; IV pumps beeping when an infusion was complete; and daylight streaming through the window. At night, the action never stopped. Las Vegas has nothing on the ICU. Nurses and therapists still came in, beepers went off, and noise often traveled from the corridor into my room.

Day after day, I had nothing to do. I couldn't get out of bed, I couldn't talk, and I couldn't use my dominant hand. My left hand was somewhat helpful but still incredibly weak. I felt like a prisoner, confined to a hospital bed, unable to express my thoughts or ask questions.

More Procedures and Setbacks

One day a doctor told me I needed a tracheostomy—a tube placed through the skin in my neck directly into my trachea, replacing the endotracheal tube. I was still on many sedatives and I didn't understand what he was saying, but Kathy tried to explain why I needed this procedure. I had to trust that they knew what they were doing.

After the tracheostomy, I learned I also needed a gastrostomy—a tube going directly through my abdominal wall and into my stomach for long-term feedings. I previously had a feeding tube that went through my mouth (and later my nose after the tracheostomy replaced the endotracheal tube) and into my esophagus and stomach. I wasn't thrilled about the gastrostomy idea, but once again I went along.

These issues were nothing compared to what I was about to face.

While I was in the ICU, one of the drugs that kept me sedated was Fentanyl, infused through my IV. The evening of the day they discontinued it, I felt worse than I'd ever felt. I panted for air, my heart raced, and my body went limp. All I wanted to do was get out of there. I sincerely thought I might die. All hope drained away. This was it—I was at the end of my life.

Suddenly, I heard the audible voice of God.

"Keep your eye on Me," He said.

Deep within, I found the strength to give praise to my Lord. I thought of nothing else but to worship Him. As I focused on the Lord, I felt removed from the thoughts of dying and gradually began to feel better. For several days I seemed stable during the daytime, but at night I started panting again and felt my heart racing. I was aware of Kathy trying to do everything she could to help me. Finally, at the end of the week, I recovered, and my vital signs stabilized.

Enduring Breathing Trials

My next challenge was the breathing trials, the times I was off full ventilator support. My body was so used to the ventilator breathing for me and my muscles were so weak that I dreaded these hours of incredible difficulty. I would look at the clock and tell myself I could last another five minutes. Then I would push myself for the next five minutes, and so on. It was a lot of work. Some days I was determined to go longer, and other days I couldn't last very long. Kathy kept telling me how important it was to breathe on my own so I could come off the ventilator. But I never thought she realized how difficult this was for me.

One night Kathy decided I should watch a funny movie so I could laugh. She thought it would help my recovery. It took me a while to focus on the film, but I eventually followed the story and enjoyed it. I remember smiling at the funny parts but never really laughing.

Two weeks after the tracheostomy, the pulmonologist said the tube needed to be changed. Shortly after this procedure, I began to bleed around the area where the tracheostomy tube was. The nurses spent the afternoon and evening putting one dressing after another on the site, but the bleeding continued.

Since I couldn't talk, I couldn't let them know the last dressing they placed wasn't doing any good; I was still bleeding. And when Kathy arrived after work, I was still bleeding. She stayed until late that night and thought the bleeding had stopped. But it resumed sometime after she left. I was lying in blood. After Kathy arrived the next morning, two pulmonologists finally stopped the bleeding. Unfortunately, I needed two units of blood to replace what I'd lost the previous day.

Now that my tracheostomy situation was stable, the breathing trials resumed. During the last week of January, I finally started to last longer during these times off the ventilator. At last, I spent most of the day off the ventilator and just went back on it to rest at night.

In the last few days of January, I improved rapidly and was completely taken off the ventilator. However, I still couldn't talk because of the tracheostomy tube.

Since I no longer needed ventilator support, the hospital moved me to a room in a step-down unit. I was so happy to leave that ICU room. In fact, I was thrilled. As they moved me to the other unit, I noticed everything in the hallway. The change of scenery was a welcome sight.

It was quieter in this unit, and I was there for only two nights before I made the big move to a Long-Term Acute Care (LTAC) facility.

Now Kathy will tell you what she experienced during this time.

Kathy

Living on a liquid diet is not ideal, and after weeks of doing so, Steve was so emaciated. One of the physicians even emphasized his "muscle wasting" to me. It was painful to see my strong and wonderful husband waste away to skin and bones. His collarbones stuck out from his shoulders. His legs looked like sticks with skin stretched over them. His knees were constantly swollen. One time the nurse placed the hospital bed in a sitting position for a few seconds, and Steve couldn't stand it. He groaned and motioned to be placed back down.

The Bible says, "We live by faith, not by what we see with our eyes" (2 Corinthians 5:7 TPT). I had to see my husband with the eyes of faith, not with my natural eyes. I refused to take a photo of Steve while he was in the ICU. In fact, I found a lovely photo of him I'd taken in October 2021, before he got sick, and made that the background on my phone. I looked at that photo all the time. I even showed it to nurses and therapists in the room, saying, "You see this? This is my husband. This is Steve. This is what he looks like. And he will look like this again." Maybe they thought I was crazy, but I wanted them to know he was a healthy, strong man who would fully recover.

While in the ICU, Steve had so much trouble with his heart rate (tachycardia) and blood pressure that they called a cardiologist for a consultation. The cardiologist said his heart was healthy and robust. He thought the lengthy illness was the cause of the tachycardia and hypertension and that it would resolve with time. A good report—finally!

Fentanyl Withdrawal, a Bleeding Scare, and Breathing Trials

Steve also went through two significant setbacks in January. One was withdrawal from Fentanyl when it was discontinued. He had tachycardia (fast heart rate), tachypnea (fast respiratory rate), hypertension, and poor oxygen saturation, and became unresponsive. The first night of this withdrawal was the worst.

First, he needed a Nipride drip (a powerful medicine that dilates blood vessels) to bring his blood pressure down. As it came down too abruptly, he became hypotensive and needed a pressor (a drug that supports blood pressure by constricting the arteries) to increase his blood pressure.

Of all the nights I spent in the hospital, this was the night I thought he might die. He was on 100 percent oxygen with oxygen saturations in the low to mid 80s. He looked terrible. But he lived, although every night that week Steve would again become tachycardic, tachypneic, and hypertensive, yet not to the degree he experienced the first night. Through this difficult time, I spoke Psalm 118:17 over Steve: "I shall not die, but live, And declare the works of the LORD."

Finally, we were past this withdrawal stage, and Steve began to improve again by the grace of God.

Since it had been two weeks since the placement of his tracheostomy tube, the pulmonologist said they needed to change the tube. The new tube would last for a couple of months. After the tube was changed, Steve started to bleed from the tracheostomy site. This was not a small amount of blood: He was covered with and lying in blood. The nurses kept putting one pressure dressing after another on the site to no avail. The bleeding continued.

About 1:00 a.m., it seemed the bleeding had slowed down or stopped, so I went home to get a few hours of sleep. When I arrived the next morning, the bleeding had started again. Steve needed two units of blood to replace what he had lost. Two pulmonologists came in to examine the site and do what was necessary to stop the bleeding. Finally, Steve could rest without bleeding profusely from the tracheostomy site.

Breathing trials resumed, and we counted each hour Steve could stay off the ventilator settings. He seemed to tire so easily, partly because his muscles were so atrophied that his respiratory effort was poor. Also, his lungs had been through a lot and were trying to heal. Steve had a short break from pneumonia after the Acinetobacter infection. However, his labs again worsened, and he developed another Pseudomonas pneumonia. I remember despising that machine that could harbor such bacteria, and I desperately wanted him off the ventilator. Once again, Steve was on another course of antibiotics. Unfortunately, pneumonia makes it challenging to endure breathing trials and wean off a ventilator.

Securing Long-Term Acute Care

During the last two weeks of January, we knew Steve couldn't stay in the hospital as he recovered; he needed to be in a longer-term facility. So I started looking for a Long-Term Acute Care (LTAC) facility. They specialize in getting patients off ventilators and on their way to rehabilitation.

As I considered which LTAC facility would be best for Steve, our insurance denied his transfer to one; they would only approve his going to a nursing home on a ventilator. We appealed the decision and were denied a second time. Then the case was to be reviewed by a panel of physicians. I thought for sure such a panel would see that my husband was a strong and healthy guy who had a full life, worked, and had no previous disability. For these reasons, I felt we had a good chance of overturning the denial.

But I was wrong! To my amazement, the insurance company would still only approve a nursing home. I could not believe what I was hearing. I told the hospital case manager I would first turn my house into a hospital and care for Steve myself. The nearest nursing home that took ventilated patients was even an hour away.

I reached out to an attorney I'd used in the past, and she gave me the name of an insurance agent who could help us. The agent referred us to another agent who was a specialist in these difficult situations. With my sister-in-law's help, I was able to change Steve's insurance during an open enrollment period at the end of January. The new insurance automatically approved the LTAC facility, and we were all set as soon as a bed was available. Although the case manager kept bringing up the nursing home idea, I knew God would not let that happen to Steve. We had come so far, and I knew my husband would recover fully.

On January 28, Steve sat on the side of his hospital bed for a few seconds. This was a milestone! By 5:30 p.m. that afternoon, he'd been off the ventilator completely (not even in assist mode) for six and a half hours and wore a trach collar. This collar goes over the tracheostomy site and blows oxygen into the tracheostomy. That night Steve went back on the ventilator to sleep as it had been a long and tiring day.

The following day, January 29, Steve was off the ventilator for twelve hours! That morning we had some challenges with clearing mucous plugs, which had decreased his oxygen level, but these resolved, and Steve continued to improve. What an answer to prayer! After all this time, Steve was weaned off the ventilator within a few days and was breathing on his own. He still had the tracheostomy, but at this point, I knew he wouldn't have it for long.

Focusing on Full Recovery

January was significant for another reason as well. While Steve was hospitalized in December, someone else we knew was also hospitalized with COVID around the same time. Unfortunately, he did not do well and passed away. As I attended his memorial in January, my heart was broken for his wife and family. I was thinking of my husband, now finally off the ventilator and improving, as I listened to the eulogies for this dear man. Since Steve wasn't near full recovery, there were still many unknowns from a natural standpoint. I had to fight the doubts that tried to take root in my mind regarding Steve's prognosis. The only prognosis I chose to believe was the one the Lord had given me: *He will make a full recovery.* That's where my focus remained.

At the service, I sat with a couple I knew from the community. The wife put her arm around me and told me not to be discouraged, that this was not the outcome my husband would have. I think she saw my tears and thought I feared Steve would pass away. I had no such fear. I wept for the widow only because I could identify with so much of the battle she went through. But I knew I would not experience the loss she now suffered. No one could change my mind about Steve's miraculous and complete recovery—not the doctors and nurses, not the case manager, not the physicians for an insurance company, not the therapists, not any other person. Steve was getting better and coming home, and that was a fact.

On January 30, Steve was transferred to a step-down unit in the hospital and was entirely off the ventilator. Glory to God! This area seemed much quieter as fewer alarms were going off all the time. I could tell Steve was glad to be out of the ICU. Then on January 31, the LTAC facility had a bed ready for his arrival on February 1 and our new insurance was in place. Miraculous!

The Power of Encouragement and Hope

Steve was more than ready to leave that hospital. Although he was going to another type of hospital, we knew they would help him recover. After all we'd been through, it was incredible to realize Steve would no longer need critical care and be in a life-threatening situation daily.

Our contact at the LTAC facility, Tasha, was an absolute angel. Her patience and encouraging words meant the world to me. When we were trying desperately to get Steve in an LTAC facility instead of a nursing home, she worked diligently to find him a bed in their facility. I had long, tearful conversations with her about what to expect during Steve's recovery. She even visited Steve when he was still in the ICU. She spoke kindly to him and assured him they would do all they could to get him back to his usual self. She was such an encouragement. She also arranged for me to stay with Steve anytime I wanted, even overnight.

Through these months of pain and anguish, I've learned the importance and necessity of giving people hope. Our faith is built on hope. Hebrews 11:1 says, "Faith is the substance of things hoped for, the evidence of things not seen" (KJV). If we have no hope, we're miserable. Our faith has nothing to grasp. Words of hope and encouragement are like gold nuggets to someone going through a challenging time.

Too often in medicine, we're callous and shallow in our interactions with patients and families. Perhaps this is a coping mechanism so we don't become depressed ourselves. However, this is not the quality of a good physician, and it's certainly not the quality of the Great Physician. There is only one Great Physician, and that's Jesus. He is our Healer. He created our bodies, and He can heal them.

12

A Walking Miracle

STEVE

We walk by faith, not by sight.

2 Corinthians 5:7

It was February 1—moving day! I was so excited to leave the hospital and enter the LTAC facility. I thought the ambulance would come in the morning, but I learned their ETA was 3:00 p.m. The day seemed to drag on. Then three o'clock came and went without anyone coming to get me. Finally, they arrived at 4:19 p.m.—yes, I know the exact time! The EMTs apologized, but they'd had an urgent run to make before picking me up.

It was a frigid winter day, and I wore a thin hospital gown, but the EMTs wrapped me in blankets before strapping me to a gurney. Once in the ambulance, I realized I didn't know how far away this LTAC facility was or how long it would take to get there. The ride was quite bumpy, much rougher than I'd expected. And it took longer than I expected because we were traveling through rush-hour traffic. I later discovered that we drove only seven miles, but it seemed to take a long time.

After we arrived and went up to the third floor, I underwent an admission process. A team of nurses and therapists were there to greet me and give me a thorough evaluation (it might have been too exhaustive). The speech therapist asked if I'd been given a speaking valve for the tracheostomy. I didn't even know there was something called a speaking valve, but it sounded great. Anything that could help me communicate would be terrific.

The following day, the speech therapist returned with the promised speaking valve. She attached it to the tracheostomy tube, and I could talk! Kathy made a video of my first words, and this is what I said:

"Now I can say what's on my mind instead of listening to everyone else. So, hi, everybody! I'm baaaaaaaack!"

Being able to talk was a huge psychological boost for me. I could finally express my opinion and not feel ignored. The speech therapist advised me not to speak so much the first few days since I hadn't used my vocal cords in such a long time. She didn't want me to create further damage to them. But I had so much to say that I talked and talked and talked even though my voice was hoarse and weak.

By that first evening, my tracheostomy was capped off, and I was entirely off oxygen with normal oxygen saturations. It was miraculous! I could breathe in room air without a ventilator or supplemental oxygen.

Two days later, on February 3, we had another snowstorm. Kathy's office was closed, and she couldn't come to see me as the roads weren't clear. It was a cold and lonely day, but I was grateful for the heated blankets at the LTAC facility. My body had difficulty regulating my temperature. At times I felt like I was freezing and shivered; other times I kicked off the covers because I felt so hot. It's hard to say if this was a normal response. Not many people recover after being on a ventilator for forty-five days. There was little precedent for my situation.

The following day, the tracheostomy tube was removed. Glory to God! The hole in my neck closed very nicely, and the scar is now barely visible. I think no one would notice it unless I pointed it out.

The LTAC facility allowed Kathy to spend the night with me, so she slept on the couch by the window. I was thrilled that she could stay, and she did every weekend.

Getting to Work

Now the work of recovery began. I stood for the first time on the day they removed the tracheostomy. But I lasted only about six seconds because I felt incredible pain in my swollen knees, and my legs were quite weak. Still the optimist, I knew I would walk again; I was just wondering how long it would take.

Again, I realized how much we take for granted. Breathing, sitting, standing, walking, eating, swallowing, talking . . . We need to understand what exceptional coordination is required for us to do each of these activities. I had lost my muscle tone, strength, balance, and coordination. Getting them back would be a long process.

I was still receiving nutrition through the gastrostomy tube, although the staff allowed me to have crushed ice. This seemed like a fantastic treat. I enjoyed the fact that I could have something in my mouth to chew.

I had a setback on February 6—trouble breathing. The facility did a chest X-ray and arterial blood gas, started me on breathing treatments, and gave me extra water in the gastrostomy tube. Thank God, I improved quickly and had no further difficulty breathing.

Learning to eat again

My next project was learning to eat again. To test my swallowing ability, I had a swallowing study on February 8. Unfortunately, I didn't pass. I had a silent aspiration during my swallowing attempts. This meant my swallowing muscles were weak, and my epiglottis couldn't protect my airway. The liquid I drank went into my trachea without me coughing or choking to get it out. I would be at risk for aspiration pneumonia if I swallowed anything in this condition. I knew for sure I didn't want to get pneumonia again.

The speech therapist explained that my facial and swallowing muscles were feeble. The attending physician told me I had damage to my epiglottis from the intubation tube. Kathy asked what we could do to correct my swallowing. The speech therapist said there were "funky" daily exercises I could do, and Kathy and my sister, Janie, kept me on track with them. The exercises were difficult and tiring, but sometimes funny.

The hardest one involved holding my tongue between my teeth while I swallowed. The facial exercises had me alternately puckering and smiling. I also had to make "eeeeee" sounds in a continuous low to high pitch. It sounded like I was doing vocal exercises with a fragile voice. I did about fifteen different exercises twice daily for ten repetitions each.

I did all the activities faithfully for two weeks. When I did the swallowing study again on February 18, I passed! I was so excited to start eating food. Little did I know there were seven levels of food textures through which I had to progress.

It began with pureed food, like baby food. And there were four levels of pureed food: slightly thick, mildly thick, moderately thick, and extremely thick. Then I advanced to level five, minced and moist foods. Next was level six, soft and bite-sized food. Seventh and last was regular food. To advance to the next level, I had to pass a test to prove I had mastered the current level of food texture without choking.

Passing the swallowing study on February 18 and starting to eat pureed food allowed me to be off the gastrostomy tube feedings. This was a significant step forward. Although I still had the tube, it was closed off and no longer the source of my nutrition.

Working on gross and fine motor skills

The physical therapists began working on my gross motor skills: sitting, standing, and walking. I started to spend more time sitting in a chair. At first, spending an hour in the chair was painful. My weight had dropped from 168 to 145 pounds during my illness, and I had no muscle mass to cushion my bony frame against the hard surface. But gradually, I could tolerate more extended periods in the chair.

The occupational therapists helped me shave, brush my teeth, and develop other fine motor skills. But my progress was limited because I didn't have the use of my right hand due to the wrist drop. I had to relearn all these skills with my left hand.

The environment at the LTAC facility seemed so much better to me than the ICU in the hospital. I started using my insulin pump and continuous glucose monitor again. I had much better control over my blood sugar with this setup. And the staff was so compassionate. They truly wanted me to get better and back to everyday life.

Although I was still on continuous monitoring for my vital signs with EKG leads, a pulse oximeter, and a blood pressure cuff, I no longer had a tracheostomy. I didn't use the gastrostomy for nutrition anymore. I was on my way to full recovery, and it felt good.

A Rehab Stay and Therapy

On February 21, I transferred to a rehabilitation hospital near the LTAC facility. This time my journey was in a van as I sat in a wheelchair. I still wore a hospital gown but was covered in warm blankets. The short trip to the rehab hospital was much more pleasant than the earlier ambulance ride.

Here, I no longer had to be on continuous monitoring. The nurses just checked my vital signs every four hours, much better than all the lead wires and cuff on my arm, which pumped up every couple of hours.

The rehabilitation hospital required me to take at least three hours of physical, occupational, and speech therapy each day, and I was excited to start this new phase of my journey to recovery. Instead of spending most of the day in bed, I had to sit in a chair or wheelchair. But I was determined to get back to normal, no matter how painful. Any improvement, even in small increments, encouraged me to continue pushing forward.

The incentive spirometer was one of the devices I used to help regain lung function. I would have to inhale slowly with this device in my mouth and fill my lungs with as much air as possible. The spirometer would register my capacity in milliliters. While at the LTAC facility, my best efforts usually measured about 500 milliliters. I thought I was doing well until I asked a respiratory therapist what my goal should be. He told me I should aim for 2,000 milliliters. What a difference!

In the rehabilitation hospital, I practiced the incentive spirometry often. I increased my spirometry to 1,250 milliliters, but I didn't get much further until I was home.

I had my therapy in the rehabilitation hospital's large gym. By February 26, I could use a seated elliptical machine and exercise for ten minutes. Then I stood between parallel bars and walked about six steps with one therapist in front of me and another following me with the wheelchair. Next, I walked sixteen feet with a walker. It was a milestone! This was the most exercise I'd had since before entering the hospital in December.

These steps seem like incredible progress when you've been in bed for three months. Since I thought I'd made significant headway, I asked the therapist how many steps I needed to take before I could go home. The answer was 150 to 200. I still had work to do.

In addition to individual therapy, I attended group therapy classes. We did marching, kicking, arm exercises, and stretches. I worked hard and even worked up a sweat at times. Some of my classmates were in post-op recovery from a knee or hip surgery. Sometimes we'd play trivia games. If you answered the questions correctly, you could do fewer exercises. This bit of competition was fun.

I enjoyed occupational therapy as I could relearn the skills of daily living I'd lost. I retrained myself to take a shower, shave, get dressed, and use utensils. For all these skills, I still had to use my non-dominant left hand since my right hand remained nonfunctional. One advantage of learning to get dressed again was that I could now wear clothes—casual pull-on pants and T-shirts. Quite an improvement over the hospital gown.

Although my knees remained swollen and painful, I still pushed myself to walk farther each day. My therapists knew I was working hard, and they were encouraging. And as I started to regain independence, my self-confidence increased. I felt more like a human than just a body struggling to survive.

The speech therapist at the rehabilitation hospital was personable, and we became friends after a few sessions. After telling him my story of survival and healing, he was astonished that I was still alive and doing so well. I shared that it was the power of prayer that kept me alive and brought me this far. I also told him I had a devoted, praying wife and many prayer warriors who fought the good fight of faith on my behalf. He replied that it was good to have such friends. We found we had similar values, and I looked forward to our sessions a few times each week.

As I progressed up the food-texture pyramid and reached level seven, I no longer needed speech therapy. However, I continued to pray for my new friend and hoped he would trust in Jesus as I did.

Real Food!

Since my meals had begun to look more like real food, I thought I'd advanced to level seven and ordered French toast for breakfast one morning. But I needed help finding it on my plate, because all I saw was a pile of brown mush that tasted terrible. I asked one of the therapists why they gave me pureed food again, and she told me I was still on level six. The only difference between level six and level seven diets was bread. Since French toast was considered bread, I couldn't have it unless it was pureed.

After my protest, they gave me a roll to try while the speech therapist watched me chew and swallow. When I didn't choke, they moved me to level seven.

To celebrate my progression to a regular diet, on the evening of March 4, Kathy and Janie brought me a delicious dinner of barbecue ribs, brisket, barbecued bologna, baked beans, Texas toast, and french fries. One jealous nurse commented on my having a "barbecue party." After all I'd been through, I felt I was entitled to such a treat.

Going Home

On March 5, the rehabilitation doctor said I was progressing better than expected, and it was time to set a date for my discharge home. I was thrilled. There would be no more hospital, LTAC facility, or rehabilitation facility. My next destination would be home sweet home. I had walked up to 110 steps with the walker and was now on a regular diet.

My discharge date was March 17, St. Patrick's Day and my dad's birthday. I was ready to do the Irish jig again, but on my feet, not lying in a bed. Working toward an actual discharge date, I began progressing even faster. One day I walked a total of 173 feet with the walker. My main limitation was the swelling and pain in my knees. And when I began to walk, I got short of breath easily, and my heart rate would quickly increase. When I pushed myself too hard, I'd have to rest a lot the next day. However, as I gained endurance, I no longer had shortness of breath or felt my heart racing when I walked. Unfortunately, my knees still hurt.

In the rehabilitation hospital, the therapists gave me different devices to help with dressing and picking things up. One was a device to help me put on my socks. I always needed help getting it to work for me, so it seemed more trouble than just bending over. Another device was a handicap grabber to pick up items off the floor. But I could pick things up more easily if I was sitting in a chair, so I never used it.

Since I was doing so well, the rehabilitation physician moved my discharge date to March 14. Glory to God! I didn't want to stay in a hospital one day longer than necessary. But I still had the gastrostomy tube in my abdomen, and the tubing was quite long. Since I was eating a regular diet, I kept asking the rehabilitation doctor to remove it. He put it off as long as he could, telling me, "Don't worry. You won't have to go home with the g-tube."

Finally, on March 13, he removed the gastrostomy tube. Praise God! I was now free from all tubes, lines, leads, and artificial connections. I could get up and walk like an average person. I'd regained all the skills for personal hygiene, although now left-handed. I'd always wanted to be ambidextrous, but such a skill had become necessary.

March 14 was my Independence Day. The hospital gave me a T-shirt to commemorate the date. It was a dream come true as the staff wheeled me out the door to the car. I left with a walker and wheelchair, and for a few weeks I used the walker to get around the house. But one day I decided it was cumbersome. Since I could carry the walker while walking, I realized I had no further need for it. The wheelchair was initially helpful when I had to get up at night as I was too tired to walk. But one day when my hand was caught between the wheel and the doorframe and I suffered a huge cut, I no longer wanted to use the wheelchair. I forced myself to get up from bed and walk on my own.

Gratitude

Kathy took a scenic route home so I could enjoy the ride, and I was thrilled to see the outside world from the front seat of our car. I have never felt so free in all my life. So often, we complain about things that genuinely don't matter, especially in the light of eternity. I've learned to be grateful and appreciate even the smallest pleasures in life: sleeping in my own bed next to my sweet wife; eating a meal of delicious home-cooked food; feeling the warm water of a shower envelop me; hugging my precious daughters; staying up late talking to Kathy; petting Boomer, our Great Pyrenees; and driving my blue Nissan Maxima.

I encourage you to think of all the things you take for granted daily and instead be grateful for them. Thank God for His grace and goodness to you every day. I believe His blessings in our lives far outweigh the difficulties, and we need to gain a new perspective on what's important to us. As Jesus said in Matthew 6:31–34 (NLT):

Don't worry about these things, saying, "What will we eat? What will we drink? What will we wear?" These things dominate the thoughts of unbelievers, but your heavenly Father already knows all your needs. Seek the Kingdom of God above all else, and live righteously, and he will give you everything you need. So don't worry about tomorrow, for tomorrow will bring its own worries. Today's trouble is enough for today.

Celebrations!

Shortly after I came home, Kathy and I had a date. Since I couldn't walk very far or navigate steps yet (even a curb), we had to be creative. We got burgers in a drive-through and sat in the car in front of the pond at Bass Pro Shop, watching the ducks. It was so much fun! We could talk and enjoy each other's company without the invasion of hospital personnel to take vital signs, change an IV, or give me a breathing treatment.

My sister had kept her Christmas tree up for me to celebrate after I came home. Although the calendar said Palm Sunday, April 10 was Christmas for me. We had a family gathering at Janie's house, with Christmas decorations and presents.

Having Christmas with my family, albeit in April on Palm Sunday, was an incredible experience after all I'd survived. God is so good! I'd come a long way. Once again, I was overwhelmed and had a wonderful time.

The following Sunday was Easter, and we had another celebration. I knew God's resurrection power was at work in my body to bring life and healing in every way. Romans 8:11 says, "Yes, God raised Jesus to life! And since God's Spirit of Resurrection lives in you, he will also raise your dying body to life by the same Spirit that breathes life into you!" (TPT). God's Spirit breathed resurrection life into my lungs and raised my dying body to life!

Recovery Continued

I found that recovery was a full-time job. I was evaluated by a physical therapist and an occupational therapist at home. The occupational therapist said I'd already met all the goals he had for me, so OT (occupational therapy) was no longer necessary. Even though I still couldn't use my right hand, I'd gained enough use of my left hand to compensate. The physical therapist came twice a week for six weeks. She had me walk all over the house and sometimes outside while following me with a roller measuring my strides. My progress depended on how my knees felt that day.

In early May, the home physical therapist said I'd met all my goals and could start driving to an outpatient physical therapy facility to continue my rehabilitation. The place was less than a mile from home, and I was thrilled to drive my car again.

Seeking a solution for my knee pain and swelling, Kathy spoke with a friend who recommended a chiropractic and naturopathic physician, Dr. Michael Taylor. Kathy's friend had seen this doctor and received treatment that helped her knee. I was excited about a therapy that didn't involve total knee replacement. We visited with this physician, and he thought he could help me. The treatments involved heat, laser, and injections in my knees. He also gave me many vitamins and supplements to aid in my recovery. This combination of therapy was excellent. My knee swelling resolved, and the pain was gone. As a result, Kathy and I expanded our thinking regarding natural medicine. We wanted to use every means God provided to aid in my recovery.

Dr. Taylor described the course of my treatment:

> We've been doing some very targeted oral nutritional medicine therapies for Steve based upon his blood work and labs. And then, additionally, we've been administering some targeted specific intravenous treatments. So it's been a combination of things. His overall quality of health has really responded and has done well. We're just so happy for him.

After seven weeks of outpatient physical therapy, I had met my goals. I was discharged from physical therapy and could go to the gym to work out. Now I needed to gain back muscle mass and endurance.

Where I Am Today

Since I enjoy walking, I began walking in the neighborhood. I'm now able to walk 1.5 miles regularly. In fact, I've walked up to 6.5 miles at one time!

As of this writing, I've also gained most of the use of my right hand—about 95 percent. I've had three electromyograms (EMGs) and nerve studies to determine where the damage lies. The first study indicated it was in my brachial plexus, the large group of nerves in the underarm. The physician who did that study noted that the nerves, although damaged, appeared to be trying to recover. The second study showed more improvement and was encouraging. The third study showed continued improvement. I went to a hand therapist twice every week, and she used electrical stimulation to test the nerves. In mid-July, during the electrical stimulation, I felt a tingling sensation in my fingertips for the first time. God has continued to heal my right hand and wrist. I went to hand therapy for about sixteen months.

Philippians 1:6 tells us, "He who has begun a good work in you will complete it until the day of Jesus Christ." I believe what the Lord told Kathy when I was in critical condition: I would recover fully. And in the Throne Room, the Lord Jesus Himself told me I would be fine. God has a purpose for me on this earth. That's why He sent me back. And I know He has a purpose for each one of us. As Jeremiah 29:11 says, "'I know the plans I have for you,' says the LORD. 'They are plans for good and not for disaster, to give you a future and a hope'" (NLT).

A Walking Miracle

Since my hospital discharge, I've had appointments with many physicians. I've seen my primary care physician, a hematologist, a pulmonologist, a neurologist, a neurosurgeon, a physiatrist, a cardiologist, a nephrologist, a naturopath, and a chiropractor. I've had X-rays, CT scans, EMGs, lung function tests, ultrasounds, and MRIs. The common denominator in every interaction with every physician has been their amazement that I'm still alive.

At my first hospital follow-up appointment with my primary care physician, Jeff, he told me he initially thought I had only a 15 to 20 percent chance of surviving. I'd spent forty-five days on a mechanical ventilator, more than anyone he'd ever heard of. During my days in the ICU, Jeff stayed in close contact with Kathy and encouraged her many times. His wife led a group of prayer warriors who prayed for me often.

When I visited the hematologist's office, he said he wasn't sure what I would look like when he entered the exam room after reading through my chart (a pretty long one). He was amazed that I was a walking and talking human being. I saw him because I'd had blood clots in the ICU. He was still quite concerned, thinking I might still have them. He ordered an ultrasound of both my legs and arms. The ultrasound was completely normal. Praise God! No more blood clots and no need for blood thinners.

The pulmonologist (lung doctor) also said that after reading through my chart, he wasn't sure what he would find when he walked into the room to see me. Of course, he was also pleasantly surprised. He did a chest X-ray at his office, and the radiology reading was "unremarkable." Unremarkable! Praise

God! That means they could find nothing wrong. This in itself was a miracle. Kathy saw my chest X-ray when I was in the hospital and later told me it looked terrible.

The pulmonologist also ordered lung function tests. While in the rehabilitation hospital, I had gotten up to 1,250 milliliters of air on the incentive spirometer. My initial goal from the respiratory therapist at the LTAC was 2,000 milliliters. Now that I was home, I could consistently inhale 3,000 milliliters of air. Doing the formal lung function test was more complicated; however, I did well. My lung capacity was only slightly below average. I had come a long way from those forty-five days on the ventilator.

I saw a neurosurgeon because of the wrist drop in my right hand and wrist. He ordered MRIs of my neck and entire right arm. There were no indications of permanent nerve damage. Praise God! However, when they did the MRI, the radiologist saw a "spot" on my right lung and asked the neurosurgeon to order a CT of my lungs. The CT was also normal, and Jeff told me it was likely background noise on the MRI.

The neurologist who did the second EMG was encouraging. He could tell that the nerves were healing in my right arm and hand. Since they heal slowly, about one inch per month, he said it might take time for me to regain full function, but it would improve. I speak God's Words of life over my right hand daily. And Kathy and I still pray every night before we go to sleep. God is restoring me completely.

When Kathy and I told our story to the naturopathic doctor, he was amazed at all I'd been through. He didn't think anyone could have survived all the complications I had. We told him it was all because of the grace of God and prayer. The second chiropractor we visited also realized that God had kept me alive for a purpose.

Kathy likes to say I'm a walking miracle. I agree. Now many others agree with us as well. Some of them are well-trained physicians; others are amazing prayer warriors. The one thing they all have in common is the recognition that it is God who healed me. Medical science gave me a slim chance of survival, but Jesus gave me a 100 percent chance.

Endurance Is Essential

The Bible tells us that with faith and patience, we inherit the promises of God: "Don't allow your hearts to grow dull or lose your enthusiasm, but follow the example of those who fully received what God has promised because of their strong faith and patient endurance" (Hebrews 6:12 TPT). We must have not only faith in the promises of God but also the patience to receive what He has promised fully. Endurance is essential.

The apostle Paul tells us, "Isn't it obvious that all runners on the racetrack keep on running to win, but only one receives the victor's prize? Yet each one of you must run the race to be victorious" (1 Corinthians 9:24 TPT). We are all in a race on this earth. We can choose to run the race well or to give up. We can believe God's promises for our lives or believe what our enemy, the devil, says. We can learn to speak what the Scriptures say or what our problems and worries tell us.

Kathy and I know from experience that nothing is impossible with God. Even when faced with critical illness, probable death, financial struggles, disability, physical and emotional pain, and incredible fatigue, we've come through with victory because of Jesus. We know we can depend on Him entirely, and He is always faithful to us.

13

Supportive Family and Friends

KATHY

For as the body is one and has many members, but all the members of that one body, being many, are one body, so also is Christ.

1 Corinthians 12:12

Getting through those overwhelming, traumatic months wasn't easy. But many people stood with us, praying and encouraging us, and without them it would have been too much to endure.

Family

It began with Stacie, our younger daughter, who as a senior in high school prayed for her dad, helped me keep the household going, and cared for our dogs. This was a difficult time for her, too, because neither Steve nor I were available for her.

Steve's sister, Janie, encouraged me, and we were in touch daily. And as you saw in earlier chapters, she visited him regularly and helped in so many ways. She often spoke to the nurses and physicians who attended him.

I have no other family close by as my parents and Steve's parents are all in Heaven. My extended family lives in Rhode Island, where I'm from, and they're all Catholic. I was in touch with my cousin Linda, a devout Catholic, and she prayed for Steve too.

A Loving Pastor

As I shared earlier, a caring pastor sent me Scripture verses almost daily. They were always just what I needed to hear. He walked me through the kidney failure, the prone positioning, the cases of pneumonia, the drug withdrawal, and the bleeding all night from the tracheostomy site with powerful Scriptures. We also had some intense phone conversations. Once in January, when I was listing all the problems we'd encountered with Steve's unyielding dependence on the ventilator and our three denials from insurance for the transfer to an LTAC facility, I was at another low point and didn't know what to do.

This pastor shared some challenging circumstances he'd walked through in the past—times when he knew he needed a miracle or else. As expected, God always came through. Something unusual would happen, and suddenly things would be better and fall into place. Our circumstances are always subject to change. God's Word, however, is not: "Jesus Christ is the same yesterday, today, and forever" (Hebrews 13:8). He is the Living Word of God.

When my heart was in great turmoil, he sent me Isaiah 26:3: "Perfect, absolute peace surrounds those whose imaginations are consumed with you; they confidently trust in you" (TPT).

A word about combatting fear:

> Whenever the thought that Steve might not make it presented itself, I forced myself to focus instead on what God's Word says about healing. As an act of my will, I turned my eyes back to Jesus and spoke His Word out loud until thoughts of life replaced thoughts of death. I was "casting down imaginations, and every high thing that exalteth itself against the knowledge of God, and bringing into captivity every thought to the obedience of Christ" (2 Corinthians 10:5 KJV).

A great battle is fought in our minds. We can choose to think positively or negatively. Proverbs 23:7 says, "As he thinks within himself, so is he" (TPT). It's so easy to think the worst, especially when physicians and others reinforce the appearance that nothing good will happen.

The question at these moments was, "Whose report do you believe?"

Our enemy, Satan, loves to intimidate us with fear, and he reveled in his ability to control massive amounts of people through panic during the days of the COVID pandemic. I can't even count how many times fear tried to grip me. It felt like a vise around my chest—you might know what I'm talking about. At those moments, I had to speak God's Word louder than before; I had to act. The Word wasn't going to speak for itself. Psalm 23 became very dear to me: "Yes, though I walk through the valley of the shadow of death, I will fear no evil; for You are with me; Your rod and Your staff, they comfort me" (verse 4).

Others from Our Church

Two more pastors from our church also called to pray with me and get regular updates on Steve: Pastor Zack and Pastor Tad. I was so happy to pray with them, knowing they cared about us. It meant so much.

Others in our church also stepped in, with our Sunday school class preparing meals for Stacie and me many times. Our church also prays over cloths every week and takes them to those too sick to attend church. Just as the early church had a custom in the book of Acts, we place the anointed cloths on the sick for healing. Acts 19:11–12 tells us, "God worked unusual miracles by the hands of Paul, so that even handkerchiefs or aprons were brought from his body to the sick, and the diseases left them and the evil spirits went out of them."

Since both these prayer cloths and the hospital sheets were white, they ended up in the hospital laundry several times. A friend at church would arrange for me to obtain another prayer cloth each time one went missing. We just prayed the missing cloths would be used to bring healing to anyone who came in contact with them.

Friends

So many friends encouraged and supported us. Here are just a few of them:

Steve and Marilyn

Earlier, we mentioned that we have some very dear friends, Steve and Marilyn, who live overseas. We met them in that Singles Bible Fellowship in the 1980s and have been close friends ever since. Ours is a rare and incredible friendship that has stood the test of time. They've stayed in our home for extended periods, and Steve and I have often taken them and their children on vacation with us. They know us well, and we know them. And as our friendship has developed, we've all learned the power of never holding on to offense, big or small. It's incredible how effective our prayers become when we let go of offense and walk in forgiveness. Even though we may see each other only every year or so, every time we pick up our friendship where we left off.

When I told Steve and Marilyn about my Steve's condition, they began praying earnestly. Marilyn said that on multiple occasions, her husband would stay up all night praying for Steve. I updated them as often as possible regarding his condition, and sometimes I asked for urgent prayer when things were going poorly. They would respond quickly and intercede for Steve with a powerful prayer. James 5:16 tells us, "The effective, fervent prayer of a righteous man avails much."

Mary

Another longtime friend from our singles group back in the 1980s is Mary. She organized a prayer group with all the "old gang," now living in many different places but still believing in intercessory prayer. She describes what that was like:

In the singles group, we believed in prayer and praying, having intercessory prayer over our singles class, and that was just a foundational thing with us. So I did that, because some of them are still here in Tulsa, and I have kept in contact with the other ones that are now out of town.

When Steve got COVID in December, I contacted roughly ten people through Facebook, let them know what was going on,

159

and asked them to pray. Kathy would text me almost every day to give me an update on Steve's condition because it wasn't like, "Oh, he's got COVID," and then you just leave it alone. Things were dramatically changing every day. It was very critical. It required a lot of prayer and intercession. And so every day she would send me something, I would forward it to the prayer team, and we just continued praying. Then Kathy would give us updates on what was happening. I would keep the team informed, and we rejoiced when we got the good news that he was healed. He's healed! And that's what the glorious thing is about prayer. Steve is a walking miracle.

Jim Camden

Steve has a friend in Colorado named Jim Camden. He worked with Jim when we lived in that state for ten years. They're both software engineers. Jim has always been a great friend and stays in touch with Steve. I contacted him when Steve went to the ICU, and he and his wife began praying regularly for him. I also texted Jim updates regularly. (You'll hear from him in a chapter ahead.)

Band mothers

I knew several mothers from when Stacie played the French horn in her school band throughout middle and high school. I contacted one of these moms, Joyce, and she started a group text to update them on prayer points for Steve. This group was so helpful in providing food for us with gift cards and an incredible care basket with many goodies.

Former professors

I contacted my favorite college professor from ORU, John. Usually, we stay in touch through homecoming, and he's known

Steve for years. John and his family prayed for Steve regularly as I sent updates. He also informed other professors who knew Steve and me, asking them to pray.

Pastor Paul and Heidi Begley

Just before he was hospitalized, Steve finished that updated version of an app I mentioned him writing for Paul Begley, an online pastor and our dear friend. When Steve was intubated, I contacted Pastor Paul and his wife, Heidi, for prayer. They not only prayed but activated their international prayer network to pray for Steve. I was thrilled to have them in our fantastic prayer chain as well.

Pastor Paul and his wife were so kind and patient regarding some problems with the software application. Steve wasn't able to get it running smoothly before his hospitalization. I was thankful for their patience and prayers as I know nothing about computer software. But deep inside I knew Steve would recover and fix the software as soon as possible.

Julie and David Yoder

Our friends Julie and David Yoder were incredible. They organized the church meal schedule and supported me so much. I would occasionally go over to their house and pour out my heart, often in tears, and they would pray with me, have food for me, and just let me talk and decompress. Their kindness was overwhelming. David was fierce in taking authority over the enemy on Steve's behalf. He was angry with the devil for daring to attack his brother in Christ. Julie said the Lord woke her to pray for Steve on many occasions. I would text her daily updates on Steve's condition, and she would send me back encouraging texts full of thoughts from God's Word.

I'll let Julie tell you their experience in her own words:

As soon as Steve went to the hospital, we just started praying for him and interceding. He was doing okay with the supplemental oxygen for a few days. My husband and I had actually taken him chocolate chip cookies because he loves them with pecans. We delivered them with earplugs because he was having difficulty sleeping in the hospital with all the noise. A few days later, his stats started not doing well, and the doctors started talking to Kathy about intubating, which was kind of strange to us all because he was breathing and talking and all of that.

And we're thinking, *Why would you want to intubate him at this point?* Kathy was like, "I don't think so." She's a doctor, obviously, so she said, "I'm not seeing the reason that he would need to be intubated at this point based on all of the stats and everything that I'm seeing."

It was on December 14 that I noted that they did finally sedate and intubate Steve, putting him into a medically induced coma. And at that point, we knew we needed to start interceding and doing some spiritual warfare because Kathy couldn't be there. Steve was there by himself in the hospital, and I told her, "The Lord's been waking me up."

At night, it was almost as if I could feel what Steve was feeling. And it was almost like a darkness or despair that I was feeling. So I would be praying in the Spirit for God to surround him, and just send angels to encamp round about him, and protect him and protect his room, and I was praying for the staff who would come in, that if any of them were not right with the Lord or there were any spiritual things attached to them, God would just take authority over anything that tried to enter that room. So that was kind of where we started.

We also did a lot of back-and-forth communication with Kathy. I was sending her messages, encouraging her and telling her, "Listen, you're going to have to stand in the gap for Steve. He can't spiritually defend himself, so to speak, because he's not conscious. But the Bible says that you two became one flesh. Because you're one flesh, you have the right to stand in the gap and take authority over whatever's going on, whatever's happening in his body, whatever darkness or whatever's trying to come against him, because you could sense it."

Our role was more to hold up Kathy's hands like Aaron did for Moses, holding up her hands and just lifting her and keeping her built up and praying for her because she was taking on the entire weight of what was going on. And so we were involved in that prayer time. And sometimes my husband would say, "Honey, we need to pray for Steve. We need to intercede right now," and we would pray and take authority over what we were sensing, and we would wait for that heaviness to lift when we were praying. I would say that went on and off for a better part of the month and a half. We also spent some time carrying meals in, and we got our Sunday school involved with doing a meal train.

Then once Kathy was able to go in with Steve, I told her and David, "Well, it just seems like the most spiritual warfare I'm doing is in the night. We need to surround Steve, because even though consciously he's not awake, his spirit can still feel the anointing and presence of God."

So David and I pulled together some worship CDs, and we got Brother Hagin's healing Scriptures. After Kathy talked to the nurse, we dropped off our CDs and Kathy had this CD player dropped off as well. We told the nurse, "We want you to put these CDs in, and we want you to put it on repeat, and we don't want it to stop. We want worship music playing while he's in there."

The nurses were really good about it! Even before Kathy could go in, the nurses were really good complying with keeping worship music playing, for which I was thankful.

When faced with my husband's life-threatening condition in the ICU, the strength of other believers who could help and encourage me was vital for me to remain strong in the faith. Friends and family flooded us with support.

I can't thank all these mighty prayer warriors I've mentioned (and others) enough for all the prayers, gifts, food, encouragement, hugs—and listening. Yes, sometimes I just needed someone to listen. I had so much to take in, and things happened rapidly in the ICU. Circumstances could change very quickly. But I had the ultimate prayer response from these amazing friends. Stacie and I were so blessed to have such tremendous support. God indeed provided for us. The battle is the Lord's; He uses people to take care of us and support us in times of need.

This is how the body of Christ is supposed to function. Colossians 2:19 says, "We receive directly from him, and his life supplies vitality into every part of his body through the joining ligaments connecting us all as one. He is the divine Head who guides His body and causes it to grow by the supernatural power of God" (TPT).

14

Doctor Friends

KATHY

As for these four children, God gave them knowledge and skill in all learning and wisdom: and Daniel had understanding in all visions and dreams.

Daniel 1:17 KJV

As a doctor, I'm blessed to have many "doctor girlfriends," women I can turn to for advice or prayer. I communicated with them daily via group texts while Steve was hospitalized. Most of them are women I attended college with at Oral Roberts University, and we try to stay in touch as much as possible.

God, in His infinite wisdom, had lined up friends for me with specialties in Internal Medicine, Emergency Medicine, and Family Medicine. Reena, Daphne, JulieMarie, and Kristina became my advisors regarding adult medicine while Steve was in the hospital. They helped me understand and critically evaluate Steve's condition every step of the way. Each of them played such a vital part in the amazing story of God healing Steve. In this chapter, I'll let some of them, and a couple of our other close doctor friends, tell you their part of our story.

My friend Dr. Daphne Kasparek, a former hospital Emergency Medicine doctor for twenty-six years and cofounder and vice president of the Dr. Lily David Institute of Health & Healing, Inc., in Sterling, Virginia, comments about our family's initial struggle with COVID:

> I had the opportunity of treating both Kathy and her husband with the antivirals and the whole different protocols that were out there. They had the usual classic cold with a cough, slight sore throat, congestion, and then just the tiredness, the exhaustion, the fatigue. I've now treated (about) 2,400 patients. So I said, "Yep, I know exactly what we need to do." We shipped off medications to them and all the vitamin supplements.
>
> Kathy and her daughter got better, but then Steve actually took a turn for the worse, and his oxygenation levels were really low. So just with outpatient therapy, he was not managing.

My friend Dr. Mary Reena Varghese, an Internal Medicine doctor, said about Steve's condition, "I can remember many times when things looked bleak." But Reena would also say to me, "He's going to be all right, Kathy."

I knew Reena was saying this as a believer, not as a physician. Often, I called her to ask a question that was too complicated to text. I know she could hear the desperation in my voice. It was so difficult to trust God when I had all this medical knowledge that often pointed to a bad outcome. Being able to text with our group of doctor girlfriends made such a difference for me.

As Reena put it, "In this chat that we have, the great majority of us are actually in the medical field. Some of us have known each other from the 1980s. We communicate with each other through the group text messaging. So when there's something going on, or a need that has come up, we just send each other messages, requesting prayer."

Daphne added from her perspective:

We all prayed every day. Many days it felt as if Steve were going to die. Our group of five or six friends, we have a common chat, and so every day Kathy would give us an update and tell us how he was doing, and we would be very specific in our prayers, each of us being different specialties. We have an Internal Medicine doctor, we have a Family Medicine doctor, and an ER doctor. So we all would gather all our knowledge and kind of tell Kathy, "Ask them about this . . . do this . . . do that."

It was days and days that she would give us detailed notes, and she was very discouraged . . . from day to day about how Steve was going to do. We would encourage her daily with Scriptures, praying with her, just supporting her through it. And she really was down. We didn't know if she was going to make it too, herself. She was sick initially, but then she got better, and then she had to be strong for Steve, plus manage a practice, plus manage home. So that was very difficult.

I think I felt like, *Lord, I don't even know where to go with this because this is way beyond what we know, even as physicians.*

Reena tells her story:

Sometime in December, Kathy sent a message out saying, "This is what's going on: Steve was diagnosed with COVID and ended up needing to be admitted." She kept us abreast of all the stuff that was happening. I'm an Internal Medicine doctor, which is a fancy name for adult medicine. Our friends—we are all from different specialties within medicine—we were texting each other to ask, "Have you done this . . . or this? And what's this value . . . and that value?"

And then Steve went . . . to the ICU, and that's when it really got a lot more concerning. When Kathy would text us and say, "This is what's going on," we would send off prayer messages, saying, "We claim healing, in Jesus' name," or "We rebuke that." We would quote Scripture verses. But at the same time, we would also be giving medical opinions on all the things that you could possibly try.

Steve had so many ups and downs. There would be some days that he would do really well, and then he would almost "crash," as we would say in medicine. Kathy would send out an emergency text message saying, "This is what's happening." And there were all the nuances with COVID, two schools of thought, and concerns that every one of us were having.

Daphne reminds us of our bond:

I met Kathy in college. She was a year or so ahead of me. She was pre-med. I was pre-med, and she was then the president of the pre-med club. And the next year we took over from her. And so I was in awe of her. She got into med school and I just kept in touch with her. And over the decades, we've been friends. She became a pediatrician. I became an Emergency Medicine doctor.

This time we all went through together was about supporting Kathy, because when you're the spouse, and you're there, and you have nothing else to give, it's very hard. And you're being told all of these negative things from people that are supposed to encourage you, but there's nobody around to do that for her. So we were remotely giving her strength, and we all saw how amazing the Lord is, and He literally has done an impossible work in Steve's life.

Reena added this about what it feels like to be a medical doctor with your own patients to care for while also dealing with someone close to you being treated medically by someone else:

It's extremely stressful when you're having to work full-time. As a physician, often, your time is not your own. When you're seeing a patient, you're trying to give them your full attention while, at the same time, realizing that you have a very dear family member who's in the ICU. On top of that, when they call you and tell you all these things, sometimes in the midst of having to deal with your own patients, you have to put aside some of those emotional feelings that you're going through, and not give in to what I call the "run around like a chicken without its head" feeling.

After work, Kathy would head to the hospital to be with Steve. And sometimes as medical providers, it's a fine balance between you stepping in and trying to practice medicine and interjecting your thoughts, while at the same time allowing those providers to do what they need to do. Or if you have a difference of opinion, thinking about how to word it properly so you're not stepping on toes.

All of these things are going through Kathy as she's dealing with this. I can only imagine how stressful it was, having to work full-time too. And then having her eighteen-year-old who was still at home, and her parents both having already gone home to be with the Lord. It would've been so stressful: early mornings, head to the hospital, then go to the clinic, and then head back to the hospital. I live on the East Coast, and Kathy is on Central Time, so I would get these messages at different times of the day and it would dawn on me, *Oh my gosh, she goes out until midnight!*

Some men were among our doctor friends as well. Dr. Douglas Holte, a Family Medicine practitioner for more than thirty years in Broken Arrow, Oklahoma, and now a physician in the Tulsa County Juvenile Detention Center, has been our friend for more than thirty years. We met him when we attended Victory Christian Center, and we became friends through a Bible Fellowship group. He found out Steve was in the hospital on a ventilator in late December 2021, and given his knowledge of the potential complications I've already described, he says, "My wife and I were praying for Steve to be able to get off the ventilator."

Daphne gives her medical insights on just how amazing and unusual Steve's COVID survival story really is:

I also have a telemedicine practice, and when this whole COVID thing hit, God really used that for me to just go into that sphere of treating COVID patients when nobody else was treating them. The key is trying to get to people early in the illness. If I've seen them within 24 to 48 hours, they get well. By God's grace, I haven't had any fatalities. Nobody's been hospitalized from my patients that I've seen, because we've usually gotten them early enough. So I can say that Steve is a miracle.

There's no question that this is God's intervention and God's plan for them. So many times in life, what we think is the worst, God brings us out [of] this sort of thing, for a testimony like this. So that was an incredible test that they went through. Each one of us, Kathy's friends, thought that Steve wasn't going to make it, that he was going to die. When he got extubated, even after the tube was out, his recovery was slow and long. And so we didn't even know if he was going to make it through that.

My practice is primarily a COVID practice now; I mean, by default I'm one of the COVID specialists. I know of two or three stories, yet there just aren't very many of recovery after that kind of ordeal. But Steve's is probably one of the most amazing stories of God's redemption and healing.

Steve and I know he's a miracle. And while it might be hard for doctors to say so, Dr. Holte was in the majority when he said:

Steve's case and recovery were definitely out of the ordinary. Not many people would have made it. On the miraculous side, I'm sure that Steve and Kathy are 100 percent on that. I wasn't there through the whole thing to see how bad he was, and what the realistic outcome was from a natural standpoint. When you have that firsthand view of how it is and you see the recovery, that could make somebody more competent to say this was miraculous. There's no way this guy could have made it except for a Divine intervention.

Dr. Michael Taylor, the friend we talked about earlier who helped treat Steve during his recovery, has been a board-certified chiropractic internist for forty-three years, one of only 130 in the United States. He supports Dr. Holte's assessment:

We take care of a whole variety of conditions. Mostly cancer, but not all. Of course, whenever we were in the midst of COVID, we were going seven days a week for several months there doing IVs and supportive care on our COVID patients.

It was a very trying time, to say the least. But we were very fortunate and blessed. All of our patients survived.

I saw Steve after he went through his ordeal and survived. He came to me and we treated him. We tried to get him back to baseline, and his baseline, with all due respect and concern, was not good.

The fact that Steve survived the ventilator . . . we'll put it this way: It never happens. If patients are on a ventilator that long, they don't make it. The fact that he survived was amazing, because most of the time, once they got put on a ventilator early on in this COVID pandemic, most patients wouldn't last but just a few days and they would pass. So he was an exceptional case from the get-go, because, I mean, it went on and on and on for forty-five days. That just does not happen. It was definitely some divine work being done there.

Steve and I are so grateful for the support we received, both physically and spiritually, from our friends in the medical community.

15

Power, Truth, and Hope

KATHY AND STEVE

The Lord gives wisdom; from His mouth come knowledge and understanding.

Proverbs 2:6

Kathy

Steve and I have learned so many things on this journey of trauma, suffering, joy, and recovery—and certainly from his visit to Heaven. But overriding all the lessons is the unfailing mercy and compassion of God. There is no person beyond His compassion, and there are no hopeless situations on this earth.

God's goodness leads sinners to repentance (Romans 2:4). No matter what you're going through, His grace is there for you. Come boldly to His throne and receive it. Hebrews 4:16

tells us, "Let us come boldly to the throne of our gracious God. There we will receive his mercy, and we will find grace to help us when we need it most" (NLT).

Of the many lessons we've learned, however, are specific ones we each want to share in the hopes of giving you hope and encouragement during your own struggles—now and in the future.

God's Word and Voice Are Powerful

Kathy

There's power in praying, speaking, and meditating on the Word of God, and the Scriptures and my prayer time were my lifeline. I spent at least one hour every morning praying for Steve; I could not imagine my life without him. And as I asked God to speak to me, I kept hearing the words "full recovery." I heard them in my spirit, deep down on the inside. And daily as I prayed, those words got stronger. So I began to say that Steve would make a full recovery—even when he kept getting pneumonia, even when they did a tracheostomy, even when they placed a gastrostomy tube in him, even when he could not endure the breathing trials, and even when the pulmonologist pointed out how much muscle wasting Steve had.

I determined there was nothing that could convince me that Steve would not recover fully. My heart and mind were set and in agreement, and my words matched what I believed.

During the time Steve's condition was critical, the Scripture I focused on most was 1 Peter 2:24, which says Jesus is the one "who Himself bore our sins in His own body on the tree, that we, having died to sins, might live for righteousness—by whose stripes you were healed." Whenever the shadow of death would appear, as an act of my will I brought my thoughts back to this

174

verse. Jesus took all our sicknesses on Himself so that we could be healed. I reminded the Lord of His Word and knew He had to fulfill that Word.

As Steve began to recover, I would meditate on Isaiah 40:29–31:

> He gives power to the weak, and to those who have no might He increases strength. Even the youths shall faint and be weary, And the young men shall utterly fall, but those who wait on the LORD shall renew their strength; they shall mount up with wings like eagles, they shall run and not be weary, they shall walk and not faint.

David Yoder, a close friend of ours for the last few years and someone you met in an earlier chapter, describes the way the Holy Spirit led him to pray:

> I just remember, I felt that shift in the prayers I was praying. I started getting really irritated at the devil. I could tell there was something else in play here that was just messing with Steve, because it happened at nighttime, when the lights were off and everybody was gone. All these bad news things happened at nighttime. In the morning, he would recover; they'd fix it and then in the daytime he'd be fine. And at nighttime again, *boom*, something else happens. There was some kind of spiritual force that was really messing with Steve.
>
> I went from, "Okay, devil, get your hands off my friend," and then I'd pray that he would recover, to coming against spiritual forces, and the enemy, and commanding him to go, and taking more of a strong stance of praying, because I realized something else was going on. It was spiritual forces tugging; they were trying to take Steve. I believe that strongly. There were so

many attempts. He could have died numerous of times, with the various things going on in there. There was something else at play here. We could see that; we could sense that. Within a few weeks there, praying back and forth, I could tell.

I believe it's probably the Holy Spirit who prompted me to say, "This stuff's happening at nighttime here. How about we get a CD player and get some music and get something charged in that air? Let's get his room charged with good spiritual things to combat whatever's coming against him." Again, because I could just feel something going on at night.

So we were praying for Steve to be released, and there was all this up and down, up and down. We were praying for probably a good month or two. Then, just shortly after that, we realized there was another group of people who were all at the same time praying for them as well. I firmly believe it was the prayers and the supplication on Steve's behalf that pulled him through and got him out of that hospital. It was not the doctors and the nurses, it was not a good treatment, it was through spiritual prayer combating those spiritual forces and telling them to get out and leave him alone.

For many months we prayed Scripture over Steve daily and followed the leading of the voice of God in what we did and how we handled things. Steve needed the strength of the Lord to fully recover, and we continually asked God for an accelerated recovery. God has been so faithful to us and given Steve a full recovery. He will be faithful to you as well when you trust in His Word.

The Marriage Covenant Is Mighty

Steve

A few months after I met Kathy, the Lord told me she was the one for me but that I would have to be patient with her as she'd been deeply hurt in the past. Being a persistent type, I was patient even when Kathy broke up with me four times. We've now been married for more than thirty years and have two beautiful daughters. It was worth being patient.

The bond Kathy and I formed as husband and wife has only grown stronger over the years. It's carried us through job changes, moves across state lines, family issues, and this battle for my health. It's most obvious in the devotion and care Kathy had for me even when I was in a coma and didn't know what she was doing.

Joel Batchelder was the best man at our wedding and has been my lifelong friend. I want to let him relate what he saw of the bond between Kathy and me during my illness:

> Kathy was totally amazing. I did not talk with her, but the messages she kept sending were totally inspiring: how much she loved Steve, how dedicated she was to stand for him in the face of everything that was going wrong. I mean, it basically looked like he would be another casualty of COVID. My thoughts were, *Steve, you couldn't have somebody love you more than Kathy in this whole deal.* And I was just totally impressed with her. Man, if I ever were in this situation, I'd want her on my side.
>
> But it all goes back to the beginning. Steve initially was not well liked by his future mother-in-law, and he was sure Kathy was the one for him. He felt he'd got a word from the Lord. So he was really going after her, and dated her quite a bit while she was in town. Then she went to St. Louis and did a residency, after she graduated from medical school. Steve would fly up there, four hundred miles away, and spend a weekend. But Kathy's mom was reluctant, because Kathy had been engaged before, and that guy had broken it off and it did not end well at all.

Steve asked her to marry him, and he gave her a ring. He showed it to me and some other friends, and I'm thinking, *Steve, are you crazy? You can't do this. Her mom has not given you her okay.* Steve actually took the ring back and held off until he could win her mom. And he finally did. I don't know exactly how—I believe her mom finally saw the kindness and love in Steve and the care that he had for Kathy.

I know that Steve was very happy when they married. I actually got to sing at the wedding; I remember that. And his brother, the one who since died in the car crash, I think he did Communion with them. So Steve was very happy. I remember that after his brother died, Steve was so glad that he had involved him in the wedding, so that he had that video of him.

Yes, it's a tremendous love story. The way Kathy fought for Steve and was there every day after work . . . And when Steve was so sick at home before he went into the hospital, Kathy was taking care of him, even when she had COVID. And she was exhausted taking care of him night and day. Actually, she told me the day that I came over to get the diabetic supplies that she had fallen from fainting, from being just exhausted. I told her, "I know we're taking care of Steve, here. Well, you've got to take care of yourself too." And she says, "Well, I'm doing what I have to do to take care of Steve." I totally believe that this love story is an incredible one.

I agree with Joel. Ours is a tremendous, incredible love story.

Kathy

Steve and I have had many trials in our life together. When we were first married, I worked eighty to one hundred hours a week—not the healthiest way to start a marriage. In fact, in a two-week period I moved, got married, and started a new job.

These items are high on the stress scale, and taken together, they really added up.

Steve was patient with me as my sleep deprivation affected our relationship. I understand why so many physicians burn out and get divorced. Medicine is a difficult taskmaster. But from the outset, we've been determined to work things out. We've had to learn to let things go. To push past disappointments. To love each other when we're hurting. And to forgive quickly.

In fact, forgiveness is an essential part of maintaining a healthy marriage. However, forgetting the past is just as important. If you don't forget an offense, you haven't really forgiven the person who offended you. This sounds like a strong statement, but I know from God's Word and much experience that if you continue to rehearse in your mind the actions that made you upset and angry, you'll never experience the entirety of God's fantastic plan for your life. When you hold on to an offense, you block His blessing from reaching you. How do I know this?

> Whenever you stand praying, if you find that you carry something in your heart against another person, release him and forgive him so that your Father in heaven will also release you and forgive you of your faults. But if you will not release forgiveness, do not expect your Father in heaven to release you from your misdeeds.
>
> Mark 11:25–26 TPT

These are the words of Jesus. If you don't release the offense, God will not forgive you for your offenses against Him. Is an offense worth hanging on to? Are you willing to risk facing God's justice for your misdeeds? Sometimes we think we're teaching people a lesson by reminding them of their shortcomings. But Jesus said, "How can you think of saying, 'Friend, let me help you get rid of that speck in your eye,' when you can't see past the log in your own eye? Hypocrite! First get rid of the log in your own eye; then you will see well enough to deal with the speck in your friend's eye" (Luke 6:42 NLT).

How do we deal with the speck in someone's eye? With love and forgiveness, just like our Father in Heaven. I believe so many marriages would be saved if we would abide by these Scriptures about forgiveness. At the root of divorce is selfishness. When we learn to become selfless, we gain the opportunity to develop amazing, lasting relationships that bless our lives in so many ways.

Focused, Specific Prayer Is Key

Kathy

Throughout the whole fight for Steve's health, I made sure to send specific requests to those praying for us. I wanted their prayers to be focused on what was happening in the moment: Pneumonia, an infection, blood pressure issues—you name it, I wanted it prayed for specifically. Our good friend Mary points out the following about being specific in prayer:

> It's helpful to me to have details. With Steve's situation, Kathy's continual updates kept us focused on "We need to pray, and how to pray." Because if we knew there was something that shifted, we needed to really press in and pray more fervently into that situation, because that was definitely an emergency. And I believe in prayer so much. People tend to throw out "I'll pray for you" and then go on about their business. And I've

180

been guilty of it too. I want to be a person of my word, because people need prayer.

Dr. Mary Reena Varghese, my friend in Internal Medicine whom you met in the "Doctor Friends" chapter, says this about the power of prayer:

I'm a person of faith and have experienced, firsthand, God's miracles in my own life. For me, prayers are an important, integral part of a person's health. You're asking the Great Physician to step in and have His hand on how things are being done in your care, in the care of the person that you're praying for. For me, the book of Revelation makes it clear that the incense is the prayers of the saints. And Jesus is presenting that before God. I call it "bombarding the Throne Room of Heaven with prayer." All healing comes from God, whether He chooses to use medical or supernatural means, the spiritual means to heal. All healing comes from God, because you can have a bad outcome with the same set of medicines and the same set of issues. One will have a good outcome. And one has a bad outcome. And I think they've done enough research to show that prayer does play a huge role in the outcome of a person's health.

If something is going on, I will notify my pastor and his wife. And they will tell the prayer group within the church, a group of women here, locally, where I live. I have been a *locum tenens* physician, which in Latin means temporary placement for a long time. I have friends in different parts of the country, also. I'll shoot off a text message, or a WhatsApp message, saying, "Pray. Please pray." I'm a firm believer in bombarding the Throne Room of Heaven with as much prayer as possible, especially depending on the scenario.

181

Jim Camden, whom Steve has known for more than two decades, is a computer programmer. They worked together at companies like Lockheed Martin on teams solving software issues. Jim says this about specific prayers:

> I got a text originally from Kathy, and that was kind of disconcerting because normally Steve contacts me. I immediately called her back, and she told me what had been happening. That was when I first found out that he was very ill, very sick, and on a ventilator and so forth. At that point in time, we just kept in constant contact with Kathy, kept in prayer, and let some friends of ours know about it to start praying for the family and for Steve.
>
> I think God listens to the prayers of His people, and I think that when it falls in His will, that He does in fact intervene for His people. I have to say that I'm a big believer in prayer, and I think He's probably the one who prompted so many people to pray to intervene in Steve's dire situation.
>
> We got in touch with Kathy several times each week. And yes, she had specific prayer requests, very specific things that we could pray for that she felt were necessary at that point in time in Steve's recovery. It was very much very specific prayers for very specific things.

Our covenant friends, Steve and Marilyn, have told us that it was easy to war with us in prayer. They were never in doubt that my Steve was going to get better and go home. In their minds, that was it. That was his only alternative, only decision. Our friend Steve goes so far as to say this of prayer:

> Steve was one of my best friends in the whole world, and I just decided, "I'm not going to lose him." There's a time when you

just put your foot down and you go to the courts of Heaven and you plead your case before the Lord. And I pled my case and said, "I need this friend, and I will not let him go. I will not let him go."

We stood our ground, and Steve Boyls is with us here today. I stood on James 5:16, which says, "The effectual fervent prayer of a righteous man availeth much." One translation says it "makes tremendous power available" that is "dynamic in its workings."

We have seen that as we have prayed. As we interceded, we perceived that tremendous power was made available. It's been dynamic. And to me, this gives hope to others that you never quit. You stay with the Word of God, stay in prayer, because even when we can't see anything with our eyes, we know that we know that we know that when we pray, tremendous power is released, and that it is dynamic in its workings. Even though we can't see it, we can't feel it, we know in our hearts that the angels are sent, the power of God is released, and that miracles are taking place.

And that's really what happens when we pray. We come into agreement with Heaven: *Lord, your kingdom come here on earth as it is in Heaven.* We become the establishing witness of God's plan and purpose here upon the earth. And miracles are released; miracles are able to take place.

The Hope of Heaven Is a Reality

Steve

Heaven is a real place, full of hope and love and life. Why did God allow me to see my family members in Heaven? I think the answer is not a religious or theological one. It was simply because of His love. I believe He wanted me to have the assurance that my family members are in Heaven. And out of His mercy and grace, He allowed me to see my dear brother, Ted, because He knew how much I missed him.

Now, what about the dogs? Seeing my dogs in Heaven goes against the religious mindset. After all, shouldn't Heaven be a solemn place with only serious pursuits? But Psalm 16:11 says, "You will show me the path of life; in Your presence is fullness of joy; at Your right hand are pleasures forevermore." This Scripture tells us Heaven is a place of joy and pleasure. Wouldn't our heavenly Father put those things we love in our eternal home for us to enjoy? Of course He would!

Our friend Mary says of my experience there:

You go to the bookstore, and there's tons of books on heaven and you say, "Oh yeah." But when you know someone who actually went to Heaven, and you know that person, it takes on a whole different meaning. It's just not a made-up story to get money. It is a real thing that Steve is passionate about wanting to share because it has made such a difference in his life, and he knows it'll make a difference in other people's lives as well.

Kathy's doctor friend Reena says of my experience:

I've not personally had any patients tell me these near-death or death experiences of going to Heaven. This is the first person whom I know personally who had that experience. You read about these experiences or hear about them, and you're not very sure. You're always a little skeptical, but when you personally know somebody . . . Kathy sent us two videos of the interview that Steve did with Pastor Paul Begley, host of *The Coming*

Apocalypse syndicated television show, and we were like, "Wow, that is amazing!"[1]

My friend Joel Batchelder had this reaction to hearing about my heavenly experiences:

> Heaven's going to be a fun place! I just loved the whole story of Steve's visit and the beauty he saw there . . . seeing his family who had gone on early. I mean, he's lost a lot: a brother, both his parents, a niece, and his in-laws. Seeing them all—that's just crazy how wonderful a reunion that must have been. So I was just elated for him that he wasn't just in limbo for that whole time he was unconscious, that he had a wonderful experience, and he had no fear. And how he was told, "Oh, we're sending you back. You're just here for a short time." Which was good for us. We were all praying our hearts out, and he was there just having a grand old time!

My friend Jim Camden reacted this way to hearing my story about Heaven:

> I'm reaching the age where there's more people over there now than there are here for me, more people I know and I love. So that's a very real thing when you're getting close to the party . . . you have a family waiting on the other side. I think that Steve's confirmation of that was significant to me, that he actually met people he knew over there. And again, the details were—his

---

1. To watch these videos yourself, see "Breaking: 'Shocking Interview Heavenly Encounter,'" YouTube video, run time 28:30, posted by Paul Begley, September 2, 2022, https://www.youtube.com/watch?v=HWzsnrWqcvw; and also "Breaking: 'Messenger from the Lord' (Stunning Info)," YouTube video, run time 28:30, posted by Paul Begley, September 9, 2022, https://www.youtube.com /watch?v=tQcBNnd04IQ&t=5s.

story was just awash in detail. Everybody was in their twenty-somethings, and they looked the way they did at that age. It just all made sense to me. That is what I would've pictured. So that touched me.

Our long-term friend Steve added, "The stories that Steve told were so similar to stories that others tell regarding their experiences in Heaven. And so, to me, that just adds credibility to Steve's story too."

Personal Integrity Validates Personal Testimony

Kathy

Personal integrity is important in validating someone's personal testimony. Integrity and reliability are some things my husband is known for, which validates his story of Heaven for all those who know him. His friend Jim Camden confirms it:

The thing about Steve is, in all kinds of different circumstances, all kinds of different levels of stress and so forth, he was always reliable in his observations. And he was always very straightforward. He's just a solid guy. He's a great friend. He's a compassionate and grounded, down-to-earth kind of guy. And you can take what he has to say as fact because there's not a bit of flamboyance or attention seeking in Steve, just not there. What you see is what you get. So I have no doubt that if Steve tells you something, it's the gospel truth as far as he is concerned. And so I have no reason to doubt him whatsoever in anything that he says about Heaven and going there. That's the kind of thing that you can take to the bank. Steve was always very truthful, straightforward, honest, candid. I can use all those words because he is just very honest, straightforward.

His story of going to Heaven really shocked me because it's like knowing somebody who won the lottery. You just never picture it happening to the people you know; that always happens to somebody else at a different state. So it was sobering and shocking just because of the uniqueness of it. It just doesn't happen to typically anybody I know; I live a pretty mundane life. And then I was very curious and thought, *I know Steve; I can go talk to him about this.* It's not something I read in the paper about somebody I don't know. I can actually go talk to him and ask him questions and so forth. So I called him up, and we had a long conversation and chatted about that.

Steve puts people at rest, at ease, right? He's very easy to talk to. I think it goes much deeper than that, however. As he related the story, the thing is, he said it like he was just matter-of-fact. In answering questions concerning some of the story's mechanics, he was just very straightforward in his answers, with perfectly logical answers. And the two of us deal in logic a lot, and software. We're both geeks, so we tend to talk in absolutes and in data, in detail. There was nothing insincere or abstract about what Steve said. It was all very concrete, very solid, very data oriented. He would say something, and then I'd ask him a question about it, and then he would give me that level of detail . . . multiple layers of detail. And if you wanted to go down and talk about further detail, he would just answer your questions and you could move down to that level of detail.

One of the things Steve talked about that kind of had me laughing was when he said, "Yeah, I'd look down, and there were my feet. I could see my feet." I mean, that's a pretty mundane thing. You'd think that you could look down and see your feet. But it was his fascination with, "I am in this strange place I've never been before. I don't know what to expect, but at least I can see my feet. At least I've got something solid to latch onto here." And it's what I would expect of Steve. I don't know how to express it other than that it was talking to someone who had literally experienced Heaven, because he just had the depth of detail, he had the answers to the questions, he could paint the picture very well. . . . Yeah, I believe Steve.

The Call to Know Jesus Christ Is Urgent

Kathy

We live in unprecedented times. Chaos is everywhere, and there's an urgent need to have a personal relationship with the living God, Jesus Christ. This has been driven home to us even more since Steve spent time in Heaven with Him. It's important for us to examine our own lives, our priorities, and our relationship with Christ. I'd like for people to examine where they stand with God, to consider where they will spend eternity if, Lord forbid, they slip away from this earth tonight.

We Have Hope at the Coming of Jesus Christ

Kathy

For those who do have a personal relationship with Jesus Christ, my husband's story presents so much hope—hope in the soon coming of Christ and hope in the eternity we will spend with Him and with each other. As Steve's friend Jim Camden puts it:

Nobody can see the future now, and God's timing is always perfect. I've seen that in my own life. I think what happened to Steve was a timing issue. The impact that Steve will have, and his book will have, and whatever else comes out of this—I think the results will speak for themselves. It's exciting to see what's really going to come out of this. And the clarity of why at this time will become clearer as time goes on.

I, too, believe that the world is not for long given the state it's in. I just see too many things happening. And I think we are in the last generation. I may not live to see it, but my children will. It's exciting because, ultimately, we will get an opportunity to see Jesus coming in glory, as He left. I'm excited about that. I would like to be here to see that. I think it'll be something unique in human history, in redemptive history.

You can resonate with everything that Steve has said if you're a believer. It is our future. Every one of us has that future as a believer, right? We're going to have that experience. And I've imagined walking the streets of Heaven so many times, trying to imagine what that would be like. I think it's the hope of all of us that we look forward to that. So I think maybe Steve's story gives us a chance to get a little bit of a taste of that.

16

Foundations of Faith

KATHY

As I think of your strong faith that was passed down through your family line. . . . It began with your grandmother Lois, who passed it on to your dear mother, Eunice. And it's clear that you too are following in the footsteps of their godly example.

2 Timothy 1:5 TPT

Earlier, I promised you a glimpse into the foundations of faith in my early life that enabled me to face the difficult days I went through while Steve was in the ICU—and unbeknownst to me, also in Heaven. The transformations God brought in my parents' lives, and in my own early on, were the building blocks on which I was able to stand while the storm of Steve's illness raged around me.

As Jesus said, "Everyone who hears these words of mine and puts them into practice is like a wise man who built his house on the rock. The rain came down, the streams rose, and the winds blew and beat against that house; yet it did not fall, because it had its foundation on the rock" (Matthew 7:24–25 NIV). I'm so grateful that my house was built upon the Rock, not sinking sand.

Let me fill you in on the faith-building process that took place in my family's life long before I met Steve.

As a young child I attended a Catholic school, and my mother, Eileen Soria, and I went to the Catholic Church. She was from a large Italian family in Providence, Rhode Island. At one point when she was single, she was moving toward becoming a nun. She joined the Third Order of St. Dominic, a lay order, and took the step toward becoming a Religious. My mother truly loved the Lord and sought after Him as best she could. But her plan, obviously, was not the one Jesus wanted her to follow, as she then met and married my father.

My father, Dr. Manuel Soria, a Filipino from a large Catholic family in the Philippines, was an agnostic psychiatrist. Although from a Catholic upbringing, he no longer attended church or practiced his faith. He preferred to play golf on Sunday mornings. He had attended a Catholic undergraduate college, San Beda College, and a Catholic medical school, Santo Tomas University, in the Philippines. After medical school, he practiced general medicine for a few years before moving to the United States in 1958, arriving in Massachusetts and doing a residency in psychiatry.

My parents met when my mother was maid of honor for her cousin, who was marrying one of my father's close friends. My father was the best man. They dated for nine months and married in 1962. They settled in Danvers, Massachusetts, and later moved to Rhode Island, where my mother grew up. Soon, I came along.

"This Is Real!"

When I was nine years old, my mother convinced my father to attend a healing service—quite a feat considering it was a religious event and a twelve-hour bus ride to Pittsburgh, Pennsylvania. My father went mostly because he saw this as a way to expose this "faith healer" minister named Kathryn Kuhlman and write a journal article about the hoax he thought she was.

My parents rode the bus with a group of Catholics known as Charismatics. They sang worship songs all the way to Pittsburgh, which my father enjoyed even though he read a psychiatry book during the trip. They arrived at the First Presbyterian Church in Pittsburgh at about 8 a.m. and had to wait outside for three hours. My father was patient with all this to humor my mother, who was into the "healing stuff."

When my parents entered the building, the atmosphere seemed charged with electricity, and the beautiful music from the choir mixed with an amazing joy and expectation. The music disarmed my father's ability to resist the love of God. As a violinist, having gone to college on a full music scholarship for violin, he was an accomplished musician. Yet he had not played music in years. Hearing the anointed music flooded him with the memories of his love for the violin.

My parents found seats in the fifteenth row from the front. When Ms. Kuhlman began to lead worship, a strange thing happened: She stopped and called out a healing that had just taken place. Scores of people came to the front and testified they had been healed, just as Ms. Kuhlman had called out. These were not minor ailments: The deaf began to hear, the lame walked, tumors disappeared, and pain of all manner vanished from the bodies of believers.

My mother was amazed and excited, but my father was still doubtful that this was real. Spurring on some of the doubt, but intriguing him nonetheless, was the way people fell backward when Ms. Kuhlman touched them. After a few times, it became too much for my father to believe. He kept trying to figure out how she did this.

While he was trying to come up with a medical explanation, Ms. Kuhlman left the platform and walked directly to my parents' row. She stood in front of the first person in the row, touched him, and then proceeded to touch every person in that row, including my parents.

As she stepped in front of them, my father braced himself. There was no way this woman was going to push him down! But instead of pushing or trying to cause a fainting episode by pressing on the carotid artery in the neck (as Daddy thought she was doing), her long fingers lightly touched their cheeks. At that moment, both my parents felt bolts of electricity course through their bodies, and they fell backward onto the pew. Ms. Kuhlman proceeded to touch everyone else in their row and then went back up to the platform.

My parents looked at each other in shock, and my mother said, "This is real!"

My father agreed. All doubts and his plan for the journal article were gone.

At the end of the service, Ms. Kuhlman presented the gospel in a clear and concise fashion. She explained that it didn't matter if you were religious or even went to church; it only mattered whether you knew Jesus as your personal Savior and Lord. She said that all one had to do was ask Jesus to be their Savior, repent of sin, and accept His finished work on the cross for complete forgiveness of sins. Then Jesus would come into your heart and life, and you would be a new person—new on the inside. When she gave the altar call, both my parents went forward, on October 6, 1972.

When their bus left Pittsburgh that day, my father put his psychiatry book down and read *I Believe in Miracles* by Ms. Kuhlman. My parents were changed forever.

A Nine-Year-Old's Perspective

When they picked me up from my grandmother's house that day, I thought there was something different about them. And in the days that followed, I would hear my father say, "Praise the Lord!" whenever anything good happened. I, of course, thought this was very strange. Then I was astonished when my father, the agnostic, went to church on Sunday morning, took us to church on Sunday night and Thursday night, and then to a Catholic Charismatic prayer meeting on Friday night. On top of this, he started a weekly Sunday afternoon prayer meeting for his patients at the state mental hospital. We had to go to this meeting too.

At first I thought my father's behavior was strange and would pass. But it never did. He wanted to know Jesus more than anything in the world. As for me, at nine years old, I loved the Lord, but I didn't know Him as intimately as my parents did—until, one week at the Sunday afternoon prayer meeting, I gave my heart to Jesus and was born again as well.

Many lessons came out of the Friday night Catholic Charismatic prayer meeting. We all went through a nine-week class called Life in the Spirit Seminar and a twelve-week class called Foundations. During the sixth week of the Life in the Spirit Seminar, we were supposed to receive the infilling of the Holy Spirit. Excitement built in our hearts, as the leaders were going to lay hands on us and pray for us to be baptized in the Holy Spirit.

Receiving Our Prayer Language

My father had received his prayer language on his own a week before they were supposed to pray for us. He woke up about 2:00 a.m., wide awake. When he couldn't fall back to sleep, he decided to pray. He prayed in English, Ilokano (his native dialect in the Philippines), Tagalog, and Spanish. He humbled himself before the Lord and asked God to forget about all his degrees and accomplishments. He wanted to approach the Father as a child and receive whatever the Lord had for him.

Suddenly, my father felt the fire of the Holy Spirit deep inside of him, and when he opened his mouth, he was speaking in another language—one he had never learned! He spoke so loudly that my mother woke up. She was excited for him, but also a bit jealous that he'd already received the gift of the Holy Spirit. Then they both prayed and rededicated themselves to the Lord.

My mother and I received our prayer languages during quiet moments of prayer at home. Although the group leaders prayed for us in the seminar, we did not speak in tongues right away. Nevertheless, we both had genuine experiences and received a gift that we would use often for the rest of our lives.

My Father's Ministry

As a Christian psychiatrist, my father was in great demand as a speaker at churches and other meetings. He joined the Full Gospel Businessmen's Fellowship International and became vice president of our chapter in Rhode Island. He was invited to speak at so many Full Gospel meetings throughout New England and upper New York State that we traveled about two weekends every month. My father's goal was to lead at least one person to Jesus every single day, and most days he did. He would tell us about the hopeless alcoholics and former criminals who accepted Jesus at his Sunday afternoon prayer meetings.

Of course, our enemy the devil was quite upset with my father's newfound faith. He tried to take his life on at least two occasions. Once, my father was parking his car at the hospital parking lot when the car lunged forward instead of stopping when my father braked. His car leaped headlong into a tree. It was totaled, but my father was unharmed.

Another time, he was sitting at his desk in the ward when an angry patient stormed in. The patient blurted out obscenities, and my father prayed in the Spirit under his breath. The patient swung his fist at him, but it hit an invisible wall six inches in front of my father's face. Once again, the man swung, and his fist hit that invisible barrier. A third time he tried to hit my father as hard as he could, but again the fist was stopped. The man was frustrated, went down the hallway, and ran across another man and beat him severely. The innocent man was taken to the Emergency Room with a broken nose and other injuries.

Watching the transformation in my father's life, the way he loved rich and poor, mentally sound and mentally troubled, I learned from him compassion and hope in the face of bleak situations. Even though he cared for the criminally insane in the forensic unit at the state mental hospital, he never complained. He prayed for his patients and cared deeply for them. He knew most of them had no one who loved them.

"Who cares for them? I do, and Jesus does," he said to me often.

God Calls Me to Medicine

At the age of eleven, I felt an intense desire to serve the Lord growing in me—and it kept growing. So I decided to ask God what He wanted me to do with my life. At the same time, my father encouraged me to become a doctor. I didn't want to be a doctor. In fact, the more he pushed the idea, the more stubborn I became.

Finally, I told the Lord I would go to medical school someday if I could go to a Christian medical school. At the end of that prayer, I said "Amen" and chuckled. There was no such thing as a Christian medical school. Now my father had to leave me alone about studying medicine. But shortly after my simple prayer, I went along on one of his speaking engagements. When we were getting ready in the hotel room that Sunday morning, the TV was on, and Oral Roberts's program came on.

"I'm announcing my plans to build a Christian medical school!" I heard him say.

My jaw dropped, and at that moment the Holy Spirit told me, *That's where I want you to go.*

Well, that settled it; I would be a doctor. But I was still only eleven years old, and a long road was ahead of me. I told the Lord He would have to help me with my grades. I was a good student at the time—A's and B's—but nothing spectacular. From that time on, however, my grades soared. I had straight A's and performed several grades ahead on standardized tests. It was all for the glory of God. I had a goal and knew what it would take to reach that goal: the Lord's help.

I applied to and was accepted into a public high school known for its strong academics. As I began to take advanced classes there, excelling got more difficult. Once again, I asked for the Lord's help, and He answered.

The idea to pray for academic help came from two men. First, my parents and I would often listen to sermons on cassette tape. One day I heard Kenneth Copeland say something spectacular and told my dad to stop the tape because I had to write it down. I wrote his words in the front of my Bible: "Jesus is made unto me wisdom. Jesus is my ability. Praise God! I do have the wisdom, I do have the ability, and I'll fulfill His will because He's called me to do so."

I made this my confession as much as possible.

Later, I heard Kenneth E. Hagin, founder of Kenneth Hagin Ministries, tell about his academic experience after the Lord healed him of an incurable disease. He said that before he was stuck in bed sick, he was a C student in school. But after he was born again and healed, he became an A student. In fact, his memory was so good that his teachers had him read a chapter in a book, close the book, and then recite the chapter word for word.

I was astonished! If God could do that for Brother Hagin, surely He could do it for me. The Scripture on which Brother Hagin stood was in the first chapter of Daniel, especially verse 17: "As for these four children, God gave them knowledge and skill in all learning and wisdom: and Daniel had understanding in all visions and dreams" (KJV).

Lessons from the Book of Daniel

The context is that Daniel and three of his Hebrew friends were taken into King Nebuchadnezzar's palace during the captivity of Israel in Babylon. There, they studied the language and history of the Chaldeans so they could be future advisors to the king. Daniel asked their teacher, a eunuch in the king's court, to allow them to maintain a diet of vegetables and water to follow their Jewish law instead of eating the king's meat (possibly offered to idols) and the wine from the king's table. The eunuch reluctantly agreed, and Daniel and his friends looked healthier than all the other children in the king's court.

Because of Daniel's obedience, he received a great blessing from God: knowledge and skill in all learning and wisdom. Daniel and his Hebrew friends were found to be ten times better than all the wise men in King Nebuchadnezzar's court.

Ten times better.

After reading this story in Daniel 1, I always flipped my Bible open and read this chapter before opening any other book to study. Then I prayed and asked for the same wisdom God gave these Hebrew children. I'd quote Daniel 1:17 daily, personalizing it. This Scripture helped me through high school, college, and medical school.

I can truly say it was God alone who helped me academically. Many times at ORU, when I couldn't understand my chemistry book, I went to a prayer room downstairs in my dorm and prayed in the Spirit for one hour. I would always tell the Lord, "Father, there's one thing we know, and we know it well, and that is that I can't do this. But your power inside me can! I'm trusting you to help me because you've asked me to go to medical school, and you're faithful to your Word." And He always was and still is faithful!

These lessons, these experiences, propelled me forward in life and equipped me for the raging storm Steve and I entered. I had no idea what was to come, but our Father God did, and He had prepared me in advance.

17

This Is for You

STEVE

If you openly declare that Jesus is Lord and believe in your heart
that God raised him from the dead, you will be saved. For it is
by believing in your heart that you are made right with God,
and it is by openly declaring your faith that you are saved.

Romans 10:9–10 NLT

Why did the Lord call me to visit Heaven and then come back
to talk about it? I've wondered that myself. Before this, I was
just going along, living my life and doing my best to serve God.
Then it all changed. Dramatically. God has a way of stopping us
in our tracks to show us the reality of His presence in our lives.

I believe the Lord transformed my life-threatening experience
into one that has forever changed me in a positive way. And
since my visit to Heaven, Jesus has told me I am a "messenger
of hope."

Did God cause my illness? Of course not! Did He use it for His glory and to give me an amazing testimony about Heaven? Yes, absolutely! I can see this in the story presented in John 9:1–2, when Jesus healed a blind man: "As Jesus walked down the street, he noticed a man blind from birth. His disciples asked him, 'Teacher, whose sin caused this guy's blindness, his own, or the sin of his parents?'" (TPT).

The disciples were quite narrow-minded in their cause-and-effect way of thinking. Look what Jesus told them and then did for the man:

> Jesus answered, "Neither. It happened to him so that you could watch him experience God's miracle." . . . Then Jesus spat on the ground and made some clay with his saliva. Then he anointed the blind man's eyes with the clay. And he said to the blind man, "Now go and wash the clay from your eyes in the ritual pool of Siloam." So he went and washed his face and as he came back, he could see for the first time in his life!
>
> John 9:3, 6–7 TPT

We have many opportunities to exercise our faith. We face trials and challenging times, and when we go through these "shadow of death" experiences, we have a decision to make: Do we practice what we believe and stand firm on the promises of God's unchanging Word, or do we complain, throw up our hands, and give up?

Second Corinthians 4:17 says, "Our present troubles are small and won't last very long. Yet they produce for us a glory that vastly outweighs them and will last forever!" (NLT). Remember who said this: the apostle Paul, who experienced tremendous persecution for the gospel. He also said, "Five different times the Jewish leaders gave me thirty-nine lashes. Three times I was beaten with rods. Once I was stoned. Three times I was shipwrecked. Once I spent a whole night and a day adrift at sea" (2 Corinthians 11:24–25 NLT).

Many ask me, "How do you know God will take care of you?"

Even before I visited Heaven, I deeply understood God's love, which He demonstrated through His Son, Jesus: "God showed His great love for us by sending Christ to die for us while we were still sinners" (Romans 5:8 NLT). Because I know Jesus intimately as my Savior and Lord, I'm confident He will take care of me in every situation. Paul reassures us of this:

> Can anything ever separate us from Christ's love? Does it mean he no longer loves us if we have trouble or calamity, or are persecuted, or hungry, or destitute, or in danger, or threatened with death? . . . No, despite all these things, overwhelming victory is ours through Christ, who loved us. And I am convinced that nothing can ever separate us from God's love. Neither death nor life, neither angels nor demons, neither our fears for today nor our worries about tomorrow—not even the powers of hell can separate us from God's love. No power in the sky above or in the earth below—indeed, nothing in all creation will ever be able to separate us from the love of God that is revealed in Christ Jesus our Lord.
>
> Romans 8:35, 37–39 NLT

Yes, this is the confidence I have in God and His great love. I know not even death can defeat me since Jesus has conquered it through His own death and resurrection. He took the penalty for our sins so we could enjoy eternal life—both a fulfilling life in this world and everlasting life in Heaven.

The spirit realm is more real than the book you hold in your hands, the chair on which you sit, and the house in which you live. It's the original realm that existed long before God created the natural, physical realm. Second Corinthians 4:18 tells us, "We do not look at the things which are seen, but at the things which are not seen. For the things which are seen are temporary, but the things which are not seen are eternal."

I sincerely pray that you, dear reader, can experience the same love and life in Christ I have, both in this world and in eternity. God created us as three-part beings—spirit, soul, and body. Your physical body will last a short time on this earth, but your spirit and soul will live forever—in either Heaven or hell. Our Father God has made a way for us to spend eternity in Heaven. That way is Jesus, who told you and me, "I am the way, the truth, and the life. No one can come to the Father except through me" (John 14:6 NLT).

Jesus asks you to accept and receive His life. He gave Himself as the ultimate sacrifice for our sins when He died on the cross for us. Man's natural tendency is not for good. We all make mistakes, beginning with our original parents, Adam and Eve. The apostle Paul explained:

Everyone has sinned; we all fall short of God's glorious standard. Yet God, in his grace, freely makes us right in his sight. He did this through Christ Jesus when he freed us from the penalty for our sins. For God presented Jesus as the sacrifice for sin. People are made right with God when they believe that Jesus sacrificed his life, shedding his blood.

Romans 3:23–25 NLT

A transformative thing happens when you believe and accept Jesus' sacrifice and ask Him to be your Savior. Your spiritual condition changes from darkness to light: "He has rescued us completely from the tyrannical rule of darkness and has translated us into the kingdom realm of his beloved Son. For in the Son all our sins are canceled and we have the release of redemption through his very blood" (Colossians 1:13–14 TPT).

This means you have God's life inside you, and all the promises God declares in His Word for His children are yours: "Anyone who belongs to Christ has become a new person. The old life is gone; a new life has begun!" (2 Corinthians 5:17 NLT).

I write these things to encourage all who know our Savior, Jesus Christ. We have an eternal home far beyond our wildest imagination, designed by God Himself. Sometimes we're tempted to complain about so many things here on earth. But after visiting Heaven and getting a glimpse into the spirit realm, I know that nothing on this earth is worth worrying or complaining about.

If you don't know Jesus, I ask you to take the next step today. Ask Jesus into your heart and life, and allow Him to transform you from the inside out into a new person, full of His life, love, and ability. Jesus stands and knocks at your heart's door: "Behold, I'm standing at the door, knocking. If your heart is open to hear my voice and you open the door within, I will come in to you and feast with you, and you will feast with me" (Revelation 3:20 TPT).

Jesus invites you to spend eternity enjoying Heaven—ultimate joy in His presence and incredible fun in everything He's prepared for you. Pray this prayer and give your life to Jesus so that you, too, can travel to the realm called Heaven and spend eternity there, discovering the amazing things God has created for us, His children:

Dear God, I acknowledge that I am a sinner and am in need of your redemption. I repent of my sins and ask Jesus into my heart and life today.

Jesus, I invite you to be my Lord and Savior. I give you my life and ask that your will be done in every area of my life. I ask you to lead and guide me, by your Holy Spirit. Thank you for my salvation. Amen.

That's all it takes! Jesus is preparing your home in Heaven now. Not only that, but you also have a fantastic future here: "'For I know the plans I have for you,' says the LORD. They are plans for good and not for disaster, to give you a future and a hope" (Jeremiah 29:11 NLT).

If you prayed this prayer, Kathy and I welcome you to God's family! And I trust that we will meet in eternity one day as well, after we've all been welcomed to Heaven.

Acknowledgments

STEVE AND KATHY

We would like to acknowledge and thank the many prayer warriors, our friends and family, who helped Kathy and Stacie while Steve was in the hospital, in both spiritual and practical ways.

Our dearest friends Steve and Marilyn Wildman prayed the prayer of faith day and night, often staying up most of the night praying in the Spirit. You are fearless in the supernatural realm, and your prayers avail much!

David and Julie Yoder likewise spent many sleepless nights praying for Steve, even nights when the Lord would awaken them to pray fiercely. Your kindness to Kathy in arranging meals for her and Stacie through our Sunday school class, letting Kathy come over late at night just to cry and pray some more, and demonstrating true agape love was overwhelming.

Mary and John Tabor arranged daily prayer with our "old gang" of friends from the 1980s when we were in a singles group together at church. Connecting us again with such wonderful people like Hope, Tracey, Joanie, Joel, and others was amazing and powerful. Thank you so much! Joel Batchelder deserves special recognition as Steve's close friend and the best man in our wedding.

Kathy's doctor friends were an invaluable resource during this incredible trial. Words of wisdom came daily from Dr. Reena Varghese and Dr. Daphne Kasparek, adult physicians who helped this pediatrician understand the unfamiliar world of the adult ICU. Thank you to Dr. JulieMarie Gerick, Dr. Kristina Earls, Dr. Jeff Chasteen, and Dr. Doug Holte, who also prayed fervently, along with their families and respective prayer groups.

Jim Camden, Steve's longtime friend and former coworker, showed such kindness and compassion to Kathy as she explained Steve's critical condition to him.

The pastoral staff at our church were amazing! One of them was in daily contact with Kathy, sending her Scriptures, praying, and, many times, just calming her soul. You touched Heaven on Steve's behalf.

Pastor Paul and Heidi Begley were outstanding examples of the love of God as they not only prayed and activated their international prayer team, but had patience with Kathy when we needed Steve to help with computer issues for their app and Kathy knew nothing about technical matters. May God bless you a hundredfold for your kindness and patience!

Kathy is forever grateful to Tasha, who helped transfer Steve to the Long-Term Acute Care facility after the ICU so that we didn't have to move Steve to a nursing home on a ventilator. Steve is so thankful for Shelly Walentiny, his hand therapist, who worked with him twice a week for fifteen months to recover the use of his right hand, which was neurologically damaged during his hospital stay.

Our thanks also go out to Joyce Halford and the band moms and Kathy's dear friend Terry for providing meals and gift cards for Kathy and Stacie when we were in need.

We are so grateful to our amazing coauthor Troy Anderson and editor Chris Dalton at Inspire Literary Group for their superb skills in helping us tell our story to the world, and Todd Burns, our literary agent, for believing in us and taking a chance. You are absolutely led by the Holy Spirit! And huge thanks to the entire team at Baker Publishing Group for seeing the hand of God at work through the telling of this supernatural story.

Finally, our deepest thanks is to our family. Steve's sister, Janie, spent every day at the hospital, praying for Steve and just being there for him. She arranged many groups of her friends to pray for him on a daily basis. Her support was invaluable! We are so grateful for our beautiful daughters, Stephanie and Stacie, who walked this journey with us, prayed, cried, felt the pain, and overcame. As a senior in high school, Stacie had to learn how to run a household, cook, and take care of the dogs while we were not available. You are both amazing and talented. We love you with all our hearts. God has great plans for your lives and for all of our lives: "'For I know the plans I have for you,' declares the Lord, 'plans to prosper you and not to harm you, plans to give you hope and a future'" (Jeremiah 29:11 NIV).

Ultimately our greatest thanks and praise is to our heavenly Father, our Lord Jesus, and the Holy Spirit: "Bless the Lord, O my soul; and all that is within me, bless His holy name! Bless the Lord, O my soul, and forget not all His benefits: who forgives all your iniquities, who heals all your diseases, who redeems your life from destruction, who crowns you with lovingkindness and tender mercies, who satisfies your mouth with good things, so that your youth is renewed like the eagle's" (Psalm 103:1–5).

Troy

I'd like to join Steve and Dr. Kathy in acknowledging all the people who were so gracious to do interviews for this book, our incredible team at Chosen Books/Baker Publishing Group—including Editorial Director Kim Bangs, our editor Jean Kavich Bloom, Senior Director of Marketing Eileen Hanson, Marketing Manager Joyce Perez, Senior Art Director Dan Pitts, and Acquisitions Assistant Kelsey Acker—our amazing literary agents Todd Burns and Stefanos Panayiotou, and the countless people who covered us in prayer as we worked on this hope-filled and inspirational book.

We'd especially like to thank all those who prayed for my wife, Irene. As we were writing *I've Been to Heaven*, she was hospitalized for seventeen days with severe COVID pneumonia, severe sepsis, acute pancreatitis, and other life-threatening conditions. A doctor told me she had only a fifty-fifty chance to live. Our family and friends, as well as the Boyls, prayed fervently for her, and we believe the Lord miraculously saved her life. It was a divine appointment that we came to know Steve and Dr. Kathy. When Irene was in the hospital, Dr. Kathy provided me with invaluable advice on how to care for a COVID patient, offering both medical guidance and spiritual encouragement during one of the most difficult seasons of our lives.

Later, while we were editing the book, Irene became severely ill again and was hospitalized for three days with acute cholecystitis. Once more, we turned to prayer, and a surgeon—who specifically asked for prayers that God would give her "steady hands and a clear mind"—successfully removed Irene's gallbladder. She later told us it had been dangerously swollen and infected, on the verge of bursting. Again, we believe God intervened to save Irene's life.

This book stands as a testimony to the power of prayer, the faithfulness of God, and the incredible way He orchestrates divine connections for His purposes.

Appendix

Healing Scriptures

KATHY

The following is a list of healing Scriptures I read daily to my husband, Steve, while he was in the hospital and afterward. These Scriptures strengthened our faith in the healing power of the Great Physician.

And the Lord God formed man of the dust of the ground, and breathed into his nostrils the breath of life; and man became a living soul. (Genesis 2:7 KJV)

The spirit of God hath made me, and the breath of the Almighty hath given me life. (Job 33:4 KJV)

Thus saith God the Lord, he that created the heavens, and stretched them out; he that spread forth the earth, and that which cometh out of it; he that giveth breath unto the people upon it, and spirit to them that walk therein . . . (Isaiah 42:5 KJV)

Thus saith the Lord GOD unto these bones; Behold, I will cause breath to enter into you, and ye shall live. (Ezekiel 37:5 KJV)

He supplies life and breath and all things to every living being. He doesn't lack a thing that we mortals could supply for him, for he has all things and everything he needs. (Acts 17:25 TPT)

Fear thou not; for I am with thee: be not dismayed; for I am thy God: I will strengthen thee; yea, I will help thee; yea, I will uphold thee with the right hand of my righteousness. (Isaiah 41:10 KJV)

Heal me, O LORD, and I shall be healed; save me, and I shall be saved: for thou art my praise. (Jeremiah 17:14 KJV)

Who his own self bare our sins in his own body on the tree, that we, being dead to sins, should live unto righteousness: by whose stripes ye were healed. (1 Peter 2:24 KJV)

Behold, I will bring it health and cure, and I will cure them, and will reveal unto them the abundance of peace and truth. (Jeremiah 33:6 KJV)

He was wounded for our transgressions, he was bruised for our iniquities: the chastisement of our peace was upon him; and with his stripes we are healed. (Isaiah 53:5 KJV)

Bless the LORD O my soul, and forget not all his benefits: Who forgiveth all thine iniquities; who healeth all thy diseases; Who redeemeth thy life from destruction; who crowneth thee with lovingkindness and tender mercies; who satisfieth thy mouth with good things; so that thy youth is renewed like the eagle's. (Psalm 103:2–5 KJV)

The prayer of faith shall save the sick, and the Lord shall raise him up; and if he have committed sins, they shall be forgiven him. (James 5:15 KJV)

Confess your faults one to another, and pray one for another, that ye may be healed. The effectual fervent prayer of a righteous man availeth much. (James 5:16 KJV)

Beloved, I wish above all things that thou mayest prosper and be in health, even as thy soul prospereth. (3 John 1:2 KJV)

A merry heart doeth good like a medicine: but a broken spirit drieth the bones. (Proverbs 17:22 KJV)

When he had called unto him his twelve disciples, he gave them power against unclean spirits, to cast them out, and to heal all manner of sickness and all manner of disease. (Matthew 10:1 KJV)

Heal the sick, cleanse the lepers, raise the dead, cast out devils: freely ye have received, freely give. (Matthew 10:8 KJV)

The LORD will take away from thee all sickness, and will put none of the evil diseases of Egypt, which thou knowest, upon thee; but will lay them upon all them that hate thee. (Deuteronomy 7:15 KJV)

My son, attend to my words; incline thine ear unto my sayings. Let them not depart from thine eyes; keep them in the midst of thine heart. For they are life unto those that find them, and health to all their flesh. (Proverbs 4:20–22 KJV)

O Lord my God, I cried unto thee, and thou hast healed me. O Lord, thou hast brought up my soul from the grave: thou hast kept me alive, that I should not go down to the pit. (Psalm 30:2–3 kjv)

I will restore health unto thee, and I will heal thee of thy wounds, saith the Lord; because they called thee an Outcast, saying, This is Zion, whom no man seeketh after. (Jeremiah 30:17 kjv)

You restored me to health and let me live. Surely it was for my benefit that I suffered such anguish. In your love you kept me from the pit of destruction; you have put all my sins behind your back. (Isaiah 38:16–17 niv)

He gives power to the weak, and to those who have no might He increases strength. . . . Those who wait on the Lord shall renew their strength; they shall mount up with wings like eagles, they shall run and not be weary, they shall walk and not faint. (Isaiah 40:29, 31 nkjv)

This is my comfort in my affliction that thy promise gives me life. (Psalm 119:50 rsv)

Lord, be gracious to us; we long for you. Be our strength every morning, our salvation in time of distress. (Isaiah 33:2 niv)

Peace I leave with you; my peace I give you. I do not give to you as the world gives. Do not let your hearts be troubled and do not be afraid. (John 14:27 niv)

For you who fear My name, the Sun of Righteousness will rise with healing in his wings. And you will go free, leaping with joy like calves let out to pasture. (Malachi 4:2 NLT)

Jesus went through all the towns and villages, teaching in their synagogues, proclaiming the good news of the kingdom and healing every disease and sickness. (Matthew 9:35 NIV)

The people all tried to touch him, because power was coming from him and healing them all. (Luke 6:19 NIV)

The LORD is my shepherd, I lack nothing. He makes me lie down in green pastures, he leads me beside quiet waters, he refreshes my soul. He guides me along the right paths for his name's sake. Even though I walk through the darkest valley, I will fear no evil, for you are with me; your rod and your staff, they comfort me. (Psalm 23:1–4 NIV)

Trust in the LORD with all your heart and lean not on your own understanding; in all your ways submit to him, and he will make your paths straight. Do not be wise in your own eyes; fear the LORD and shun evil. This will bring health to your body and nourishment to your bones. (Proverbs 3:5–8 NIV)

Be anxious for nothing, but in everything by prayer and supplication, with thanksgiving, let your requests be made known to God; and the peace of God, which surpasses all understanding, will guard your hearts and your minds through Christ Jesus. (Philippians 4:6–7 NKJV)

Heal me, O LORD, and I shall be healed; save me, and I shall be saved, for You are my praise. (Jeremiah 17:14 NKJV)

Worship the LORD your God, and his blessing will be on your food and water. I will take away sickness from among you. (Exodus 23:25 NIV)

The righteous cry out, and the LORD hears them; he delivers them from all their troubles. The LORD is close to the brokenhearted and saves those who are crushed in spirit. (Psalm 34:17–18 NIV)

When Jesus came down from the mountainside, large crowds followed him. A man with leprosy came and knelt before him and said, "Lord, if you are willing, you can make me clean." Jesus reached out his hand and touched the man. "I am willing," he said. "Be clean!" Immediately he was cleansed of his leprosy. (Matthew 8:1–3 NIV)

Gracious words are a honeycomb, sweet to the soul and healing to the bones. (Proverbs 16:24 NIV)

Praise the LORD, my soul, and forget not all his benefits—who forgives all your sins and heals all your diseases, who redeems your life from the pit and crowns you with love and compassion. (Psalm 103:2–4 NIV)

KATHY BOYLS, MD, is a board-certified pediatrician and a lactation consultant with a bachelor of science in Biomedical Chemistry from Oral Roberts University and a doctor of medicine degree from ORU Medical School. She has been in practice for over thirty years, both in private practice and urgent care.

As a result of her experience with Steve's prolonged illness, Dr. Kathy has a passion to help children with chronic illness through a functional medicine approach, using natural therapies to treat the root cause of illness as well as to promote overall health. After his hospitalization, Steve and Kathy sought out natural therapies to support his recovery from an extremely weakened state. Because of the success she saw with this approach, Dr. Kathy encourages you to be open-minded and always well informed regarding your health options. She emphasizes the importance of treating the whole person—spirit, soul, and body—to promote true health, which ultimately comes from our Creator. "He is the Lord that healeth thee!" (Exodus 15:26 KJV). God's Word is the best medicine available!

Dr. Kathy is a Fellow of the American College of Pediatricians and a member of the Medical Academy of Pediatric and Special Needs. Her functional medicine practice is Freedom Pediatrics (FreedomPeds.com).

———————— Connect with Kathy ————————

DrKathy@SteveAndKathyB.com

SteveAndKathyB.com   @HeavensMessenger

STEVE BOYLS is a software engineer with more than thirty-five years of experience. He has a computer science degree from the University of Tulsa; has worked in the oil and gas industry, telecommunications, and for the Department of Defense; and today he has his own software development company. Since recovering from his prolonged ICU stay, Steve developed a keen interest in stem cell activation for healing and wellness through an affordable photobiomodulation technology. His company is Lightforce Unlimited.

Steve's passion is to share his Heaven experience, communicating details of this blessed hope we have in Christ: "But as it is written: 'Eye has not seen, nor ear heard, nor have entered into the heart of man the things which God has prepared for those who love Him.' But God has revealed them to us through His Spirit. For the Spirit searches all things, yes, the deep things of God" (1 Corinthians 2:9–10).

Steve and Kathy—best friends who have been married more than thirty years—live in Tulsa, Oklahoma. They have two grown daughters, Stephanie and Stacie, and an energetic husky named Winnie. Steve enjoys watching professional baseball and college football and is an avid Red Sox fan. In his downtime, he enjoys listening to jazz, rock, or classical music and getting regular exercise. Kathy is an avid reader, studying natural remedies to help children heal and stay well. She is involved in several intercessory prayer groups and loves to teach about health as well as faith, merging wellness for the whole person—spirit, soul, and body.

———————— Connect with Steve ————————

Steve@SteveAndKathyB.com

SteveAndKathyB.com   @HeavensMessenger

TROY ANDERSON is a Pulitzer Prize–nominated investigative journalist, bestselling author, vice president and COO of Battle Ready Ministries, founder and president of the Inspire Literary Group, founder of Prophecy Investigators, and cofounder of Revelation Watchers. During his three-decade career in journalism, he has worked as a reporter, bureau chief, and editorial writer at *The Los Angeles Daily News*, *The Press-Enterprise*, and other newspapers, and he served as executive editor of *Charisma* magazine and Charisma Media.

He is also the coauthor of the national bestsellers *The Babylon Code*, *Trumpocalypse*, *The Military Guide to Armageddon*, *The Military Guide to Disarming Deception*, *Revelation 911*, and *Your Mission in God's Army*, and the author of the national bestseller *The Trump Code*.

Troy and his family live in Irvine, California.

———————————— **Connect with Troy** ————————————

TroyAnderson.us

InspireLiterary.com

ProphecyInvestigators.com

RevelationWatchers.com

BattleReadyMinistries.org

@TroyAndersonWriter

@TroyMAnderson

@TroyMAnderson